iGlobal
Math Workbook

Texas Edition
Power Practice for School, Home, and Tutoring

iGlobal™
Educational Services
Believe. Inspire. Transform.

iGlobal Math Workbook

To order, contact
iGlobal Educational Services,
PO Box 94224,
Phoenix, AZ 85070

Website: www.iglobaleducation.com

Fax: 512-233-5389

HOW TO USE THIS PRACTICE WORKBOOK

iGlobal Educational Services created this math resource to help you practice math skills. Please work through the practice problems and then check your work at the back of the book where the answer keys are located.

These practice worksheets should be used to supplement strong and viable curriculum that encourages differentiation for all diverse learners. They can be used at home, in tutoring sessions, or at school.

TABLE OF CONTENTS

REPORTING CATEGORY 1 (READINESS)
NUMBER AND OPERATIONS

PROBLEM SET 1

3.2A Numbers are made up of digits in the same way words are made up of alphabet s. A number is composed by adding those values together.

For example: $2,000 + 500 + 50 + 6 = 2,556$

A number is decomposed when you start with the number and you give the place values of each digit in the number.

For example: $2,556 = 2,000 + 500 + 50 + 6$

---

1. Chris used a place-value chart to write a number.

Thousands	Hundreds	Tens	Ones
3	5	8	6

   Which shows the same number?

   A. $300 + 50 + 6$
   B. $300 + 500 + 6$
   C. $3,000 + 80 + 6$
   D. $3,000 + 500 + 80 + 6$

2. A coffee shop sold four thousand, nine hundred and seventy-four cups of tea during June. What is this number in expanded form?

   A. $4,000 + 900 + 70 + 4$
   B. $4,000 + 900 + 7 + 4$
   C. $4,000 + 90 + 70 + 4$
   D. $400 + 90 + 7\,4$

3. Which of the following means 21 thousands, 7 hundreds, 9 tens, and 3 ones?

   A. 21,793
   B. 2,793
   C. 2,173
   D. 2,193

4. Corey tried to write the number 60,650 in expanded form:

   $$60,000 + 600 + 50$$

   Which change would make Corey's answer correct?

   A. $60,000 + 600 + 50 + 0$
   B. $60,000 + 0,000 + 600 + 50 + 0$
   C. $60,000 + 650$
   D. $60,000 + 6 + 50$

5. Lara used a place-value chart to write a number.

Ten Thousands	Thousands	Hundreds	Tens	Ones
5	0	9	5	6

Which shows the same number?

A. $50,000 + 1000 + 900 + 50 + 6$

B. 50,950

C. 51, 950

D. 50, 956

PROBLEM SET 2

3.2A Numbers are made up of digits in the same way words are made up of alphabet s. A number is composed by adding those values together.

For example: $2,000 + 500 + 50 + 6 = 2,556$

A number is decomposed when you start with the number and you give the place values of each digit in the number.

For example: $2,556 = 2,000 + 500 + 50 + 6$

---

1. Which number is equal to the following figure?

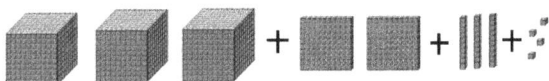

   A. 300,234
   B. 30,234
   C. 33,230
   D. 3,234

2. Decompose the number: 5,789

   A. $5,000 + 789$
   B. $5000 + 780 + 9$
   C. $5000 + 700 + 80 + 9$
   D. $5 + 7 + 8 + 9$

---

3. Find the place value of digit 6 in the number:

   76,072

   A. 2
   B. 4
   C. 1000
   D. 6000

4. Tessa's mom has given her 5 hundred dollar notes, 7 ten dollar notes and 9 one dollar notes. What is the total amount does Tessa get?

   A. 500709
   B. 5709
   C. 579
   D. 957

---

5. What is the place value of 9 in the number:

   1,190,360

   A. 9 tens
   B. 9 hundreds
   C. 9 thousands
   D. 9 ten thousands

PROBLEM SET 3

3.2B describe the mathematical relationships found in the base-10 place value system through the hundred thousands place.

1. Destiny has underlined four numbers. Which of the numbers that is underlined has a place value of 600?

   A. 263
   B. 565
   C. 680
   D. 566

2. Austin is one of the fastest growing cities in America and it has a population of 693, 875. How many ten thousands are in this number?

   Record your answer and fill in the bubbles on the following grid. Be sure to use the correct place value.

3. John is preparing his project report on Mt. Everest. One of the interesting facts that he is writing in his report is that the height of Mt. Everest is twenty-nine thousand, thirty-five feet. How is this number written in standard form?

   A. 290,035
   B. 2,935
   C. 29,035
   D. 29,350

4. In 5870, which digit is in the hundreds place?

   A. 5
   B. 8
   C. 7
   D. 0

5. The Empire State Building is located in New York City. The total height of the building, including the lightning rod, is 1,454 feet. What is another way to write this number?

A. $1,000 + 400 + 50 + 4$

B. $1,000 + 40 + 50 + 4$

C. $1,000 + 400 + 5 + 4$

D. $1 + 4 + 5 + 4$

PROBLEM SET 4

3.2B describe the mathematical relationships found in the base-10 place value system through the hundred thousands place.

1. Which does **NOT** show the number 4, 701?

A. 4 thousand, seven hundred one
B. 47 hundred one
C. 47 hundred and one
D. 3 thousand, 17 hundreds one

2. The table shows the number of tickets that were sold for a music concert.

Day of Week That Tickets Were Sold	Number of Tickets
Monday	963
Tuesday	865
Wednesday	2680
Thursday	8166
Friday	8500

Which day the number of tickets were sold that had a 6 in the ones' place?

A. Monday
B. Tuesday
C. Wednesday
D. Thursday

3. Anna lives in San Francisco and wants to visit her grandmother in New York. The driving distance between San Francisco and New York is two thousand, nine hundred six miles. What is the value of this number in standard form?

Record your answer and fill in the bubbles on the following grid. Be sure to use the correct place value.

⓪	⓪	⓪	⓪	⓪	⓪	⓪	⓪
①	①	①	①	①	①	①	①
②	②	②	②	②	②	②	②
③	③	③	③	③	③	③	③
④	④	④	④	④	④	④	④
⑤	⑤	⑤	⑤	⑤	⑤	⑤	⑤
⑥	⑥	⑥	⑥	⑥	⑥	⑥	⑥
⑦	⑦	⑦	⑦	⑦	⑦	⑦	⑦
⑧	⑧	⑧	⑧	⑧	⑧	⑧	⑧
⑨	⑨	⑨	⑨	⑨	⑨	⑨	⑨

4. Calix is trying to find his friend's house number. His friend said that he lived in building 7, which represents the thousand's place. Which could be a possible apartment number for Calix's friend?

A. 1977
B. 1870
C. 1711
D. 7891

5. When Sandra wrote down the number of how many pennies she had saved in expanded form, she wrote the value of the digit 4 as 4000.

In the number below does the digit 4 have a value of 4000?

A. 4371
B. 545
C. 480
D. 564

PROBLEM SET 5

> 3.2C Represent a number on a number line as being between two consecutive multiples of 10; 100; 1,000; or 10,000 and use words to describe relative size of numbers in order to round whole numbers.

1. Which number in multiple of 10 comes between 990 and 1010 on a line number?

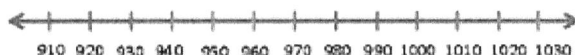

910 920 930 940 950 960 970 980 990 1000 1010 1020 1030

A. 995
B. 1020
C. 1040
D. 1000

2. Which point would best represent the number 632 on the following number line?

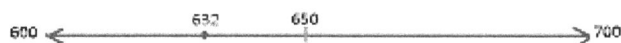

600 ← 632 650 → 700

A. approximately 600
B. approximately 700
C. approximately 650
D. none of these

3. What is the missing number in the number line?

950 960 980 990

A. 940
B. 965
C. 970
D. 980

4. In the following number line the dot will represent which number?

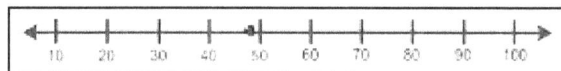

10 20 30 40 50 60 70 80 90 100

A. about 10
B. about 40
C. about 50
D. about 100

5. Which point would best represent the number 423 on the following number line?

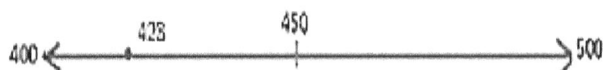

400 ← 423 450 → 500

A. approximately 400
B. approximately 500
C. approximately 450
D. none of these

PROBLEM SET 6

3.2C Represent a number on a number line as being between two consecutive multiples of 10; 100; 1,000; or 10,000 and use words to describe relative size of numbers in order to round whole numbers.

1. In the following number line, the dot will represent which number?

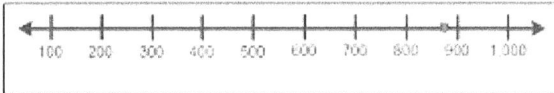

100 200 300 400 500 600 700 800 900 1.000

A. about 700
B. about 850
C. about 800
D. about 900

2. Find the missing number in the number line and write in the box?

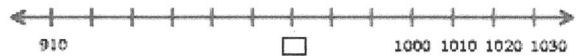

918 ☐ 1000 1010 1020 1030

A. 990
B. 980
C. 970
D. 916

3. Maxime's grandparents are 8890 miles away from her place. Which number line below has a red dot showing Maxime's grand parents' place distance?

A.

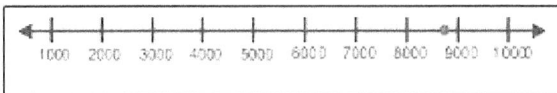

1000 2000 3000 4000 5000 6000 7000 8000 9000 10000

B.

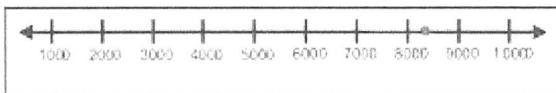

1000 2000 3000 4000 5000 6000 7000 8000 9000 10000

C.

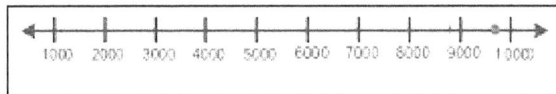

1000 2000 3000 4000 5000 6000 7000 8000 9000 10000

D.

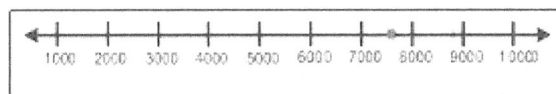

1000 2000 3000 4000 5000 6000 7000 8000 9000 10000

4. A famous dictionary contains 8282 pages. Which point would best represent the number 8282 on the following number line?

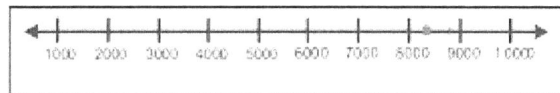

1000 2000 3000 4000 5000 6000 7000 8000 9000 10000

A. approximately 7000
B. approximately 10000
C. approximately 9000
D. approximately 8000

5. Aliya read 48 pages on Monday. The following day she read only 10 pages. Which point would best represent the total number of pages read on the following number line?

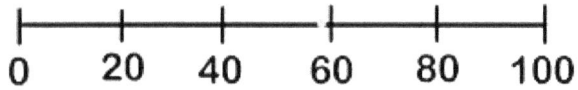

```
├────┼────┼────┼────┼────┤
0    20   40   60   80  100
```

A. about 20
B. about 40
C. about 60
D. about 80

PROBLEM SET 7

> 3.2D Compare and order whole numbers up to 100,000 and represent comparisons using the symbols >, <, or =.

1. Arrange these numbers in increasing order:

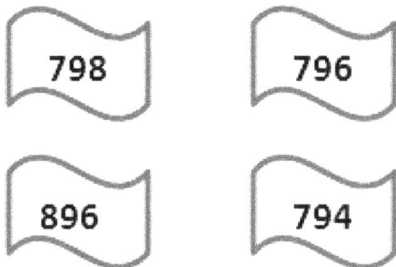

798   796

896   794

A. 794 > 796 > 798 > 896
B. 896 > 798 > 796 > 794
C. 896 > 796 > 794 > 798
D. 794 < 796 < 798 < 896

2. An art and craft teacher kept the record of how many craft works her students completed.

Craft work done	
Craft work done	Number of students
0	3
1	1
2	6
3	4
4	10
5	5

How many students did the 3 or less than 3 craft works?

A. 4
B. 14
C. 10
D. 29

3. Put these amounts of money from least to greatest.

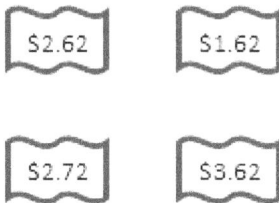

$2.62 $1.62

$2.72 $3.62

A. $1.62 < $2.62 < $2.72 < $3.62
B. $1.62 < $2.72 < $2.62 < $3.62
C. $3.62 < $2.62 < $2.72 < $1.62
D. $1.62 > $2.62 > $2.72 > $3.62

4. There are 3289 birds in x bird sanctuary and 1438 more birds join during summer. In Y bird sanctuary there are 4893 birds, in Z bird sanctuary 4978 and in W bird sanctuary 4983. In which sanctuary there are more birds?

A. X
B. Y
C. Z
D. W

5. James walked 697 steps on Sunday. On Monday he walked 31 steps more than Sunday. Which sign will you use in the box to compare?

Sunday's steps [ ] Monday's steps

A. <
B. >
C. =
D. None of these

PROBLEM SET 8

> 3.2D Compare and order whole numbers up to 100,000 and represent comparisons using the symbols >, <, or =.

1. A famous celebrity signs this many autograph each day. On which date did the celebrity sign the fewest autograph?

Autograph signed	
Monday	4891
Tuesday	8491
Wednesday	1982
Thursday	891
Friday	9841

A. Monday
B. Tuesday
C. Thursday
D. Friday

2. A farmer wrote down how many kilograms of strawberries were sold in the past 4 days.

Straberries	
Day	Kilograms
Saterday	1934
Sunday	2347
Monday	2353
Tuesday	3354

On which day were the most strawberries sold?

A. Saturday
B. Sunday
C. Monday
D. Tuesday

3. In a cupcake baking competition there were four participants. Who baked more cupcakes?

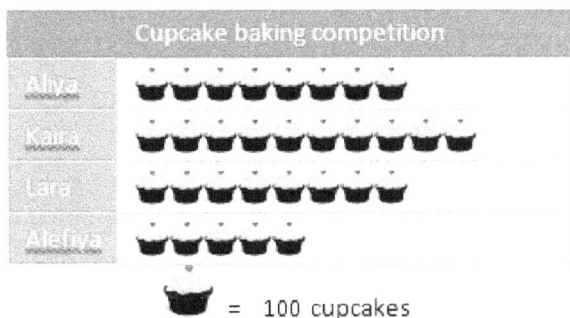

Cupcake baking competition

Aliya

Kaira

Lara

Alefiya

= 100 cupcakes

A. Aliya
B. Kaira
C. Lara
D. Alefiya

4. A DVD rental shop has 5416 movie DVDs, 4516 kid's movie DVDs, 6896 music DVDs and 6986 games DVDs. What type of DVD is more?

A. Movie
B. Kid's movie
C. Music
D. Games

5. On a number line where does 8849 lie?

A. ← 8894
B. → 9803
C. Between 2894 and 6803
D. Between 8869 and 8898

3.3A Represent fractions greater than zero and less than or equal to 1 with denominators of 2, 3, 4, 6, and 8, using concrete objects and pictorial models including.

1. Maria bought 4 popsicles. She gave 2 to her younger brother. What fraction of the popsicles had she given?

A. $\frac{1}{3}$

B. $\frac{1}{4}$

C. $\frac{1}{2}$

D. $\frac{2}{3}$

2. A girl has 12 dolls. 4 of her dolls have blond hair. What fraction of the dolls do not have blond hair?

A. $\frac{2}{3}$

B. $\frac{3}{6}$

C. $\frac{1}{2}$

D. $\frac{1}{3}$

3. What fraction of the shape is red?

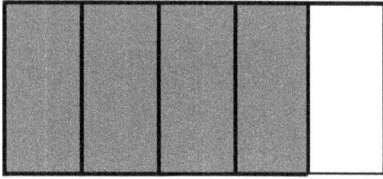

A. $\frac{1}{3}$

B. $\frac{4}{5}$

C. $\frac{1}{4}$

D. $\frac{3}{4}$

4. What fraction of the shape is purple?

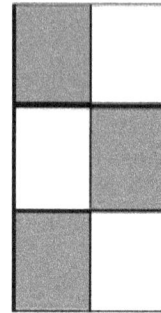

A. $\frac{1}{3}$

B. $\frac{1}{4}$

C. $\frac{1}{2}$

D. $\frac{2}{3}$

5. Which shape shows fraction ?

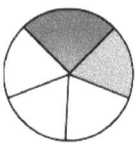 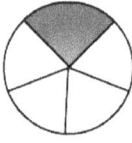 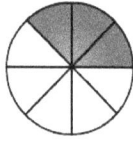 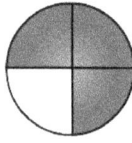

A　　　B　　　C　　　D

3.3A Represent fractions greater than zero and less than or equal to 1 with denominators of 2, 3, 4, 6, and 8, using concrete objects and pictorial models including.

---

1. Which shape shows the fraction ?

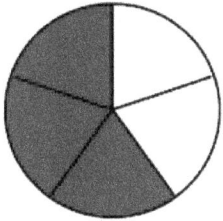
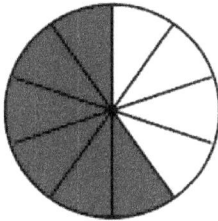

A   B

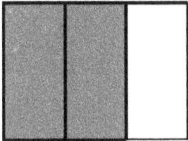
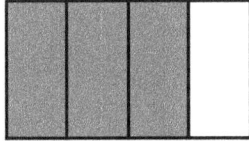

C   D

2. There were 10 pieces of cakes on the table. Jill ate 4 from that and left remaining pieces for his younger sister. What fraction of the cakes was left on the table?

A. $\frac{1}{2}$

B. $\frac{3}{5}$

C. $\frac{1}{5}$

D. $\frac{2}{3}$

3. Erin watered ¾ of the garden in the morning. Which of the following figures match with his work?

A.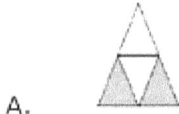

B.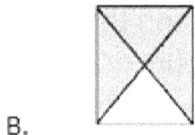

C.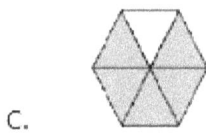

D.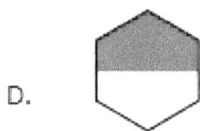

4. Which point represents the location of ½ on the number line?

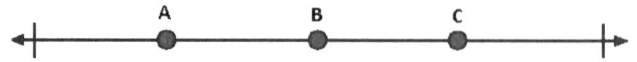

A. A
B. B
C. C
D. None of these

5. Amanda has painted 4/5 of the wall. Which of the following figures match with her work?

A.

B.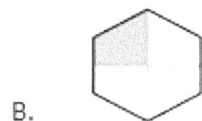

C.

D.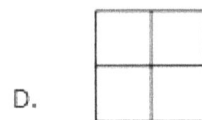

> 3.3B Determine the corresponding fraction greater than zero and less than or equal to 1 with denominators of 2, 3, 4, 6, and 8 given as a specified point on a number line.

1. Which number line shows a colored segment with a length of ¼ ?

A.

B.

C.

D.   None of these

2. Mom bought 10 apples and 10 oranges. What fraction of the fruits shown on the number line are apples?

A. $\dfrac{1}{2}$

B. $\dfrac{1}{3}$

C. $\dfrac{1}{4}$

D. $\dfrac{2}{5}$

3. The coach has 3 basketballs, 6 baseballs, and 3 soccer balls. What fraction of the balls are soccer balls?

A. $\dfrac{1}{2}$

B. $\dfrac{1}{3}$

C. $\dfrac{1}{5}$

D. $\dfrac{1}{4}$

4. Alex has 3 blue pens and 6 yellow pens. What fraction of the pens is blue?

A. $\dfrac{1}{2}$

B. $\dfrac{1}{3}$

C. $\dfrac{1}{4}$

D. $\dfrac{2}{5}$

5. Which number line shows a colored segment with a length of **2/5**?

A

B

C

D. None of these

PROBLEM SET 12

3.3B Determine the corresponding fraction greater than zero and less than or equal to 1 with denominators of 2, 3, 4, 6, and 8 given as a specified point on a number line.

1. is what part of 1?

A. One half
B. Two half
C. One third
D. One fourth

2. What fraction is represented by the dot in the following number line?

A. $\dfrac{2}{8}$

B. $\dfrac{6}{8}$

C. $\dfrac{5}{6}$

D. $\dfrac{4}{5}$

3. Which number line shows a colored segment with a length of ?

D. None of these

4. Alan and Paul bought a large pizza to share. Alan ate 5/8 of the pizza. What fraction of the pizza was left for Paul?

A. $\dfrac{2}{8}$

B. $\dfrac{4}{5}$

C. $\dfrac{5}{6}$

D. $\dfrac{3}{8}$

5. What fraction is represented by the letter C in the following number line?

A. $\dfrac{3}{5}$

B. $\dfrac{1}{3}$

C. $\dfrac{1}{5}$

D. $\dfrac{3}{4}$

> *3.3C Explain that the unit fraction 1/b represents the quantity formed by one part of a whole that has been partitioned into b equal pats where b is a non-zero whole number.*

1. Sara painted some shapes. Now, she wants to know which picture does not show equal parts. Which picture should Sara select?

A.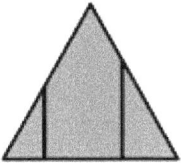

B.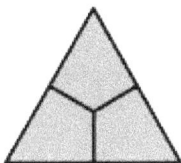

C.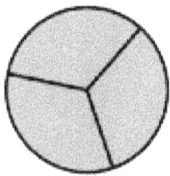

D.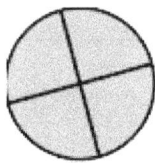

2. Three children are playing with a few shapes. Which shape can be divided equally amongst the children?

A.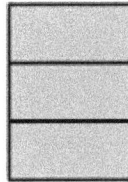

B.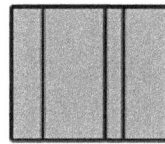

C.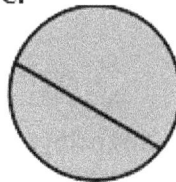

D.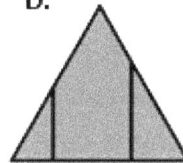

3. John wants to count the parts of lemon slice; what fraction will he choose for the whole slice?

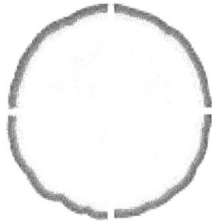

A. $\frac{4}{4}$

B. $\frac{8}{4}$

C. $\frac{2}{8}$

D. $\frac{1}{4}$

4. Lisa's birthday cake was divided in to 3 equal parts. What fraction should be chosen for the whole cake?

A. $\frac{3}{3}$

B. $\frac{1}{3}$

C. $\frac{1}{4}$

D. $\frac{3}{2}$

5. Melony is celebrating her birthday. She ordered pizza for her friends. Which figure shows fourth?

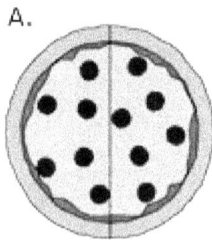

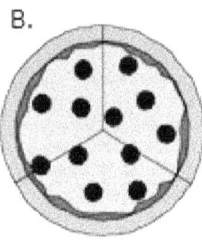

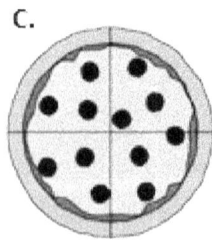

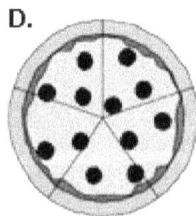

A.

B.

C.

D.

PROBLEM SET 14

3.3C Explain that the unit fraction 1/b represents the quantity formed by one part of a whole that has been partitioned into b equal pats where b is a non-zero whole number.

1. Shade 1 part of the rectangle.

When 1 part of the rectangle is shaded, what fraction is shaded?

A. $\frac{2}{3}$

B. $\frac{1}{4}$

C. $\frac{1}{5}$

D. $\frac{1}{3}$

2. Use the fraction bar to complete the sentences below.

The fraction bar has _____ equal parts.

A. 0
B. 2
C. 3
D. 1

3. There were 12 slice of cake. Diana ate 6 slices. Which given fraction will be used to describe it?

A. $\frac{3}{2}$

B. $\frac{1}{4}$

C. $\frac{1}{2}$

D. $\frac{1}{3}$

4. In a class test, Amyra, is asked to use a rectangular figure and determine which part of the rectangle is one-fourth of the whole. Which answer should Amyra select?

A. $\frac{3}{2}$

B. $\frac{1}{4}$

C. $\frac{1}{3}$

D. $\frac{1}{2}$

5. Richards' mother asked him to get 1/3 piece of any of the cookies available in the cake shop. Which of the given cookie will Richard choose to take back home?

A.

B.

C.

D.

PROBLEM SET 15

3.3D Compose and decompose a fraction a/b with a numerator greater than zero and less than or equal to b as sum of parts 1/b.

1. What fraction of the bar is shaded?

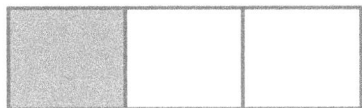

A. $\frac{1}{2}$

B. $\frac{1}{3}$

C. $\frac{1}{4}$

D. None of these.

2. What fraction of the square is shaded?

A. $\frac{1}{2}$

B. $\frac{1}{3}$

C. $\frac{2}{3}$

D. $\frac{1}{4}$

3. What fraction of the bar is shaded?

A. $\frac{1}{2}$

B. $\frac{1}{3}$

C. $\frac{2}{3}$

D. $\frac{2}{5}$

4. What fraction of the square is shaded?

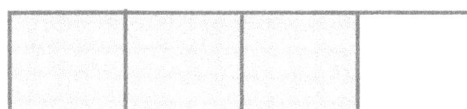

A. $\frac{3}{4}$

B. $\frac{1}{3}$

C. $\frac{2}{3}$

D. $\frac{1}{2}$

5. Ishan has $20. He wants to buy a toy car that costs $5. What fraction of her money he needs to spend to buy the toy?

A. $\frac{1}{5}$

B. $\frac{2}{5}$

C. $\frac{1}{4}$

D. $\frac{3}{3}$

3.3D Compose and decompose a fraction a/b with a numerator greater than zero and less than or equal to b as sum of parts 1/b.

1. Sam brought a bag of marbles and found that 5 of 25 marbles in the bag are blue. What fraction of Sam's marbles is blue?

A. $\frac{1}{5}$

B. $\frac{2}{5}$

C. $\frac{1}{4}$

D. $\frac{3}{3}$

2. Jim, Diana, and Lauria painted their bedroom. Jim painted of the wall. Diana painted of the wall and Lauria painted of the wall.

What fraction of the wall is painted?

A. $\frac{3}{5}$

B. $\frac{2}{5}$

C. $\frac{4}{5}$

D. $\frac{4}{15}$

3. Amanda is little bit confused and wanted to know that = ? Help her in finding.

A. + +
B. + +
C. +
D. All of the above.

4. Aliya is having a party with her 2 friends. They order one party size submarine sandwich and it is cut into 12 equal parts. They eat the entire sandwich, but each person has a different number of parts as shown in the figure below by different color. What is one way the sandwich was shared?

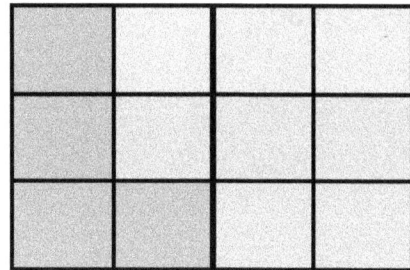

A. + +
B. + +
C. + +
D. + +

5. Lara ordered a whole pizza cut into 8 pieces. She divided the pizza among three friends(including her and not necessary everyone gets equal) as shown in the figure using different shades. Which of the following combination makes true?

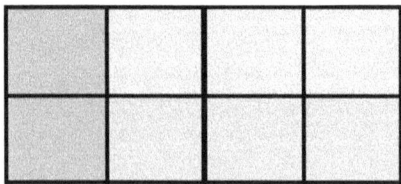

A. + +
B. + +
C. + +
D. None of these

PROBLEM SET 17

3.3E Solve problems involving partitioning an object or a set of objects among two or more recipients using pictorial representations of fractions with the denominators of 2, 3, 4, 6, and 8.

1. Jasmine bought some popsicles for her friends. What fraction of the popsicles is blue?

A. $\dfrac{1}{6}$

B. $\dfrac{2}{6}$

C. $\dfrac{2}{4}$

D. $\dfrac{3}{6}$

2. Sofiya got some balloons to decorate the class. What fraction of the balloons is yellow?

A. $\dfrac{4}{7}$

B. $\dfrac{2}{6}$

C. $\dfrac{2}{7}$

D. $\dfrac{3}{7}$

3. In the evening children got their own ball to play in the garden. What fraction of the balls is orange?

A. $\frac{1}{6}$

B. $\frac{2}{6}$

C. $\frac{4}{6}$

D. $\frac{3}{6}$

4. Alina bought 12 soft toys. She gave of the toys to her sister. How many toys did Alina give to her sister?

A. 3
B. 4
C. 5
D. 2

5. Aliya has some marbles in her desk. What fraction of the marbles is blue?

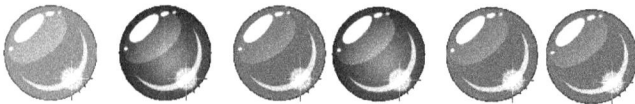

A. $\frac{1}{6}$

B. $\frac{2}{6}$

C. $\frac{3}{4}$

D. $\frac{3}{6}$

PROBLEM SET 18

3.3E Solve problems involving partitioning an object or a set of objects among two or more recipients using pictorial representations of fractions with the denominators of 2, 3, 4, 6, and 8.

1. Eric has collected 6 strawberries from the garden. He ate 3 of them. What is the fraction of strawberries that Eric has eaten?

A. $\frac{1}{2}$

B. $\frac{1}{6}$

C. $\frac{2}{4}$

D. $\frac{3}{6}$

2. Jacob got some cars on his birthday. What fraction of the cars is red?

A. $\frac{4}{7}$

B. $\frac{5}{6}$

C. $\frac{2}{7}$

D. $\frac{3}{7}$

3. What fraction of the circle is green?

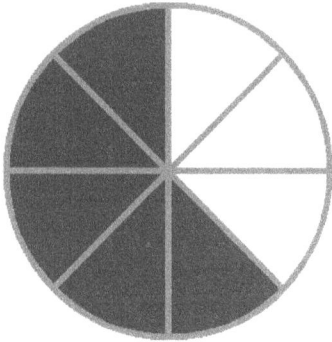

A. $\dfrac{1}{8}$

B. $\dfrac{2}{8}$

C. $\dfrac{5}{8}$

D. $\dfrac{3}{7}$

4. Eric ordered a pizza. He ate one piece only. The picture shows the part of the pizza that is left.

What fraction of pizza is left?

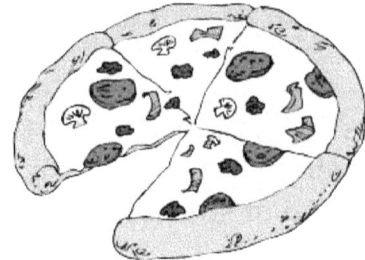

A. $\dfrac{4}{5}$

B. $\dfrac{2}{5}$

C. $\dfrac{2}{4}$

D. $\dfrac{3}{6}$

5. Alan had 10 stickers. He gave of the stickers to his friends last week. How many stickers did Alan give to his friends last week?

A. 3
B. 4
C. 5
D. 2

PROBLEM SET 19

3.3F Represent equivalent fractions with denominators of 2, 3, 4, 6, and 8 using a variety of objects and pictorial models including number lines. Equivalent fractions are different fractions that represent the same value.

1. Riya got one pizza and ate half of the pizza. Which fraction is equal to half?

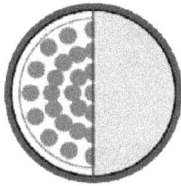

A. $\frac{1}{2}$

B. $\frac{1}{3}$

C. $\frac{1}{4}$

D. $\frac{3}{4}$

2. What fraction does the dot represent on number line?

0 ——————————————— 1

A. $\frac{1}{2}$

B. $\frac{1}{5}$

C. $\frac{1}{4}$

D. $\frac{3}{4}$

3. Which shaded area shows the fraction $\frac{1}{5}$?

A.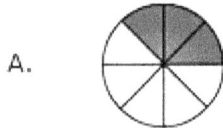

B.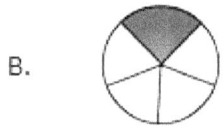

C.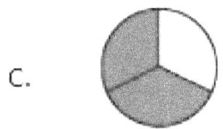

D.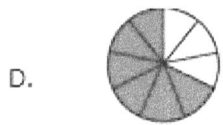

4. There were 6 girls in a swimming pool. 4 got out. What fraction of the girls was left?

A.

B.

C.

D.

5. Which fraction is equivalent to ?

A. $\frac{2}{5}$

B. $\frac{3}{5}$

C. $\frac{5}{8}$

D. $\frac{6}{8}$

PROBLEM SET 20

> 3.3F Represent equivalent fractions with denominators of 2, 3, 4, 6, and 8 using a variety of objects and pictorial models including number lines. Equivalent fractions are different fractions that represent the same value.

1. Write the correct symbol in the box (= or ≠).

2. Write the correct symbol in the box (= or ≠).

3. What fraction of the pentagon is shaded?

A. $\frac{2}{5}$

B. $\frac{3}{5}$

C. $\frac{5}{8}$

D. $\frac{3}{4}$

4. Which of the following option is equal to?

A.

B.

C.

D.

5. One-third of the 12 children went for picnic. Which shaded areal denotes the number?

A.

B.

C.

D.

PROBLEM SET 21

3.3G Explain that two fractions are equivalent if and only if they are both represented by the same point on the number line or represent the same portion of a same size whole for an area model.

1. Karina got of cake. Aliya got of pizza.

Katrina got of sandwich. Which fraction is less?

A. $\frac{1}{2}$

B. $\frac{1}{3}$

C. $\frac{1}{6}$

D. All are equal

2. Mom made 3 bowls of pasta. She put extra cheese on 1 of them. Which fraction image is equal to the fraction of pasta with extra cheese?

A
B
C
D

3. Which fraction is equivalent to the fraction shown in the picture?

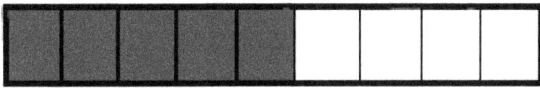

A. $\dfrac{10}{18}$

C. $\dfrac{5}{4}$

B. $\dfrac{5}{9}$

D. $\dfrac{10}{12}$

A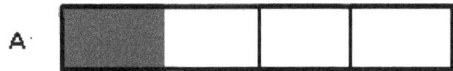

B

C

D

4. Which of the following fractions is NOT equivalent to the fraction shown in the picture?

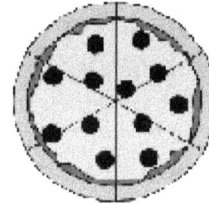

A. $\dfrac{3}{7}$

B. $\dfrac{1}{2}$

C. $\dfrac{6}{6}$

D. $\dfrac{4}{6}$

5. Sam got a square paper and folded the paper in four equal parts. Then he colored some parts.

Help him to know which of the following fraction is equivalent to the above picture?

A

B

C

D

PROBLEM SET 22

3.3G Explain that two fractions are equivalent if and only if they are both represented by the same point on the number line or represent the same portion of a same size whole for an area model.

1. Look at the picture below:

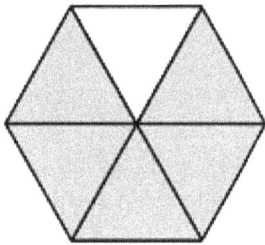

Which of the following fraction is equivalent to the shaded part of above picture?

A

B

C

D

2. Which of the following two fractions are equivalent on the following line?

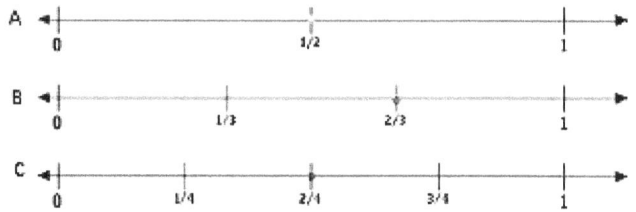

A. A and B
B. B and C
C. A and C
D. None of these

3. 6 students went to the zoo. 5 of them saw the penguins. Look at the following images and tally with the fraction of the students saw the penguins?

A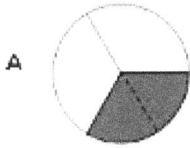

B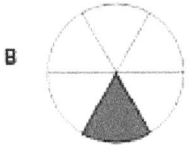

C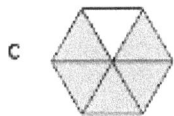

D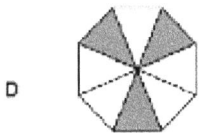

4. There are 4 cars parked in the basement. 2 of the cars are red. Which of the following fraction of shape shows the above fraction?

A

B

C

D

5. Mom made 8 pieces of toast. She put butter on 3 of them. Which of the following shape is equal to the fraction of toast with butter?

A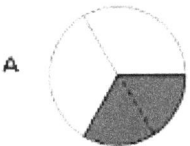

B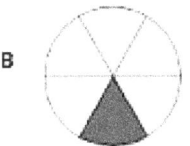

C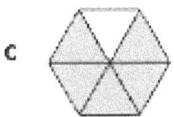

D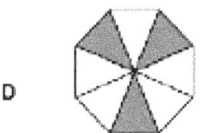

PROBLEM SET 23

3.3H Compare two fractions are having the same numerator or denominator in problems by reasoning about their sizes and justifying the conclusion using symbols, words, objects, and pictorial model. Fraction is a part of a whole. It is written as numerator divided by denominator.

1. Which fraction is greater?

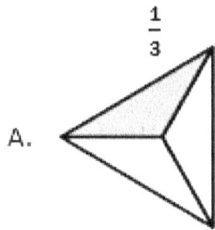

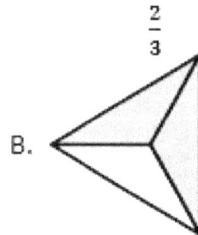

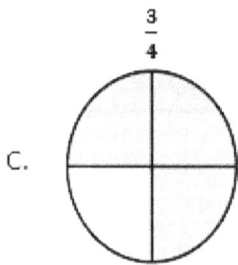

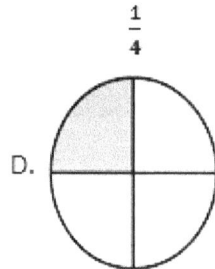

A. $\dfrac{1}{3}$

B. $\dfrac{2}{3}$

C. $\dfrac{3}{4}$

D. $\dfrac{1}{4}$

2. Which fraction is less?

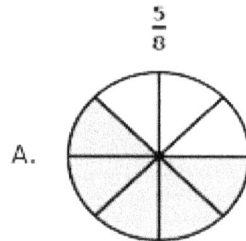

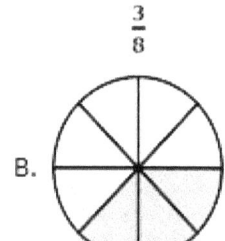

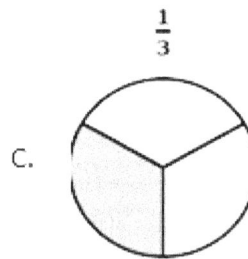

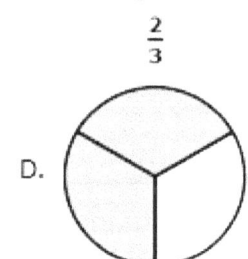

A. $\dfrac{5}{8}$

B. $\dfrac{3}{8}$

C. $\dfrac{1}{3}$

D. $\dfrac{2}{3}$

3. Siara wants to put these fractions from least to greatest order. Please help her.

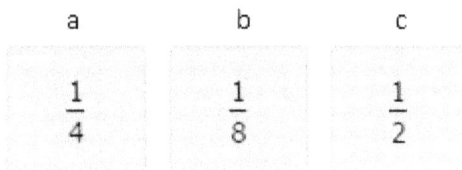

a	b	c
$\dfrac{1}{4}$	$\dfrac{1}{8}$	$\dfrac{1}{2}$

A. abc
B. bca
C. cab
D. bac

4. Brynell's midterm exams are next week. Till now she has studied portion of science, portion of math, portion of English, and portion of french. Which is the subject brynell is least prepared for?

A. French
B. English
C. Math
D. Science

5. On the given number line, which fraction is closer to zero?

A. $\dfrac{2}{4}$

B. $\dfrac{1}{4}$

C. 1

D. $\dfrac{3}{4}$

PROBLEM SET 24

3.3H Compare two fractions are having the same numerator or denominator in problems by reasoning about their sizes and justifying the conclusion using symbols, words, objects, and pictorial model. Fraction is a part of a whole. It is written as numerator divided by denominator.

1. On the given number line, which fraction is closer to one?

$$\xleftarrow{\qquad} \underset{0}{|} \quad \underset{\frac{1}{8}}{|} \quad \underset{\frac{2}{8}}{|} \quad \underset{\frac{3}{8}}{|} \quad \underset{\frac{4}{8}}{|} \quad \underset{\frac{5}{8}}{|} \quad \underset{\frac{6}{8}}{|} \quad \underset{\frac{7}{8}}{|} \quad \underset{1}{|} \xrightarrow{\qquad}$$

A. $\dfrac{3}{8}$

B. $\dfrac{1}{8}$

C. $\dfrac{7}{8}$

D. $\dfrac{5}{8}$

2. In a football match, John alone made 3 goals out of 6. What fraction will you use to describe the goals John made?

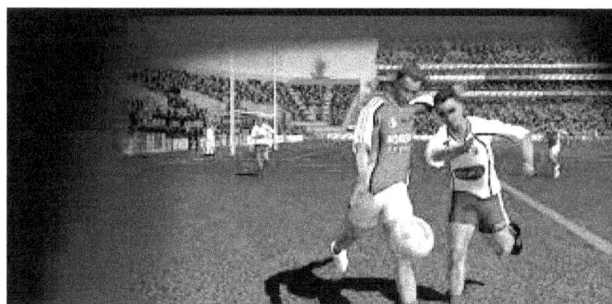

A. $\dfrac{2}{3}$

B. $\dfrac{1}{4}$

C. $\dfrac{1}{2}$

D. $\dfrac{1}{3}$

3. Rachel is making orange ginger cookies. Which ingredient will she need the most from the given list of ingredients?

A. Cup sugar
B. Cup butter
C. tea spoon salt
D. Cup flour

4. In a school math test, Ibrahim is suppose to arrange the given fractions from greatest to least order. How will he do?

a	b	c
$\dfrac{1}{10}$	$\dfrac{1}{2}$	$\dfrac{1}{5}$

A. abc
B. bca
C. cab
D. bac

5. In the first week of school;
   On day one- of the class was present;
   On day two- of the class was present;
   On day three- of the class was present;
   On day four- of the class was present;
   On which of the above day, attendance of students was the least?

A. Day One
B. Day Two
C. Day Three
D. Day Four

PROBLEM SET 25

> **3.4l Determine if a number is even or odd using divisibility rules.**

1. A factory produces 2453 bulbs in the month of January, 1527 bulbs in February, 3646 bulbs in March and 2793 bulbs in April. In which month, did the factory produce an even number of bulbs?
   A. January
   B. February
   C. March
   D. April

2. In an election, 5124 people voted for Peter, 4499 people for Alex and 3682 people for Mike in a town. Which of the above contestant got an odd number of votes?
   A. Peter
   B. Alex
   C. Mike
   D. None of the above

3. The price of a sofa set is $9372. The price of a dining table is just half of the price of the sofa. Which of the following option is correct?
   A. The price of the sofa is an odd number
   B. The price of the sofa is an odd number
   C. The price of the dining table is an even number
   D. None of these

4. Samantha has 20 cookies. She distributed cookies among her 3 friends. Ria got one fourth of the cookies, Tina got half of the cookies and Katrina got one fourth. Who got an even number of cookies?
   A. Ria
   B. Tina
   C. Katrina
   D. None of these

5. A factory manufactured 4685 toys in three weeks. The production in first week was 1445 toys and in second week 8152 toys. Which number of toys is considered to be even?
   A. The production of first week
   B. The production of second week
   C. The total production of first and second week
   D. None of these

PROBLEM SET 26

3.4l Determine if a number is even or odd using divisibility rules.

1. A shopkeeper has 2425 boxes of pencils, out of them 950 are of red pencils, 650 are green and rest are yellow. Which color has an odd number of pencils?

  A. Red
  B. Green
  C. Yellow
  D. None of these

2. There are 4,503 people signed up for the talent show. The flyer says that there is an even number of people signed up for the talent show. Is this flyer correct?

  A. No, because 4 is an even number.
  B. No, because 3 is an odd number.
  C. Yes, because 5 is an odd number.
  D. Yes, because 0 is neither an even or odd number.

3. There are 1968 bags of sugar, 6487 bags of wheat and 2622 bags of rice being donated to a local food bank.

Which type of grain has an odd number of bags being donated to a local food bank?

  A. Sugar
  B. Wheat
  C. Rice
  D. None of these

4. Linda bought a coat for $2265 and a Jacket for $2150. She gave $5000 to the shopkeeper. Which number is considered to be an odd number?

  A. The cost of the coat
  B. The cost of the jacket
  C. The amount given by Linda to shopkeeper
  D. None of these

5. An apple tree has 62 ripe apples on it in the month of April. Heavy rain shows happened the following month and there were 13 more apples that became ripe.

Which number is considered to be an even number?

  A. The number of apples in the month of April
  B. The number of apples in the next month
  C. The total number of apples of both months
  D. None of these

REPORTING CATEGORY 2 (READINESS) COMPUTATIONS & ALGEBRAIC RELATIONSHIPS

PROBLEM SET 27

3.4A Solve with fluency one-step and two-step problems involving addition and subtraction within 1,000 using strategies based on place value, properties of operations, and the relationship between addition and subtraction.

1. What number has 5 tens and 1 fewer one than tens?

A. 59
B. 55
C. 54
D. 49

2. What number has 8 tens and 1 fewer one than tens?

A. 89
B. 87
C. 84
D. 99

3. Which sign makes the statement true?

$$(15 + 1) + 1 \boxed{} 19 - 2$$

A. <
B. >
C. =
D. None of these

4. Which sign makes the statement true?

$$(16 + 5) + 20 \boxed{} 17 - 4$$

A. <
B. >
C. =
D. None of these

5. 14 brown baskets and 26 green baskets are on the truck. How many more green baskets are there than brown baskets?

A. 30
B. 10
C. 40
D. 12

PROBLEM SET 28

3.4A Solve with fluency one-step and two-step problems involving addition and subtraction within 1,000 using strategies based on place value, properties of operations, and the relationship between addition and subtraction.

1. 60 apples were in a basket. 25 were sold. How many apples were not sold?

   A. 35
   B. 30
   C. 85
   D. 25

2. There were 13 roses in the vase. Julia picked some more roses from her flower garden. There are now 21 roses in the vase. How many roses did she pick?

   A. 7
   B. 10
   C. 9
   D. 8

3. There are 31 apple trees currently in the garden. Gardener will plant more apple trees today. When the gardener is finished his work there will be 53 apple trees in the garden. How many apple trees did the gardeners plant today?

   A. 21
   B. 22
   C. 32
   D. 23

4. There were 37 students in a bus. 13 got off the bus. How many students are on the bus? Which of the following option used place value addition?

   A. $30 - 10 = 20 : 7 - 3 = 4$: Total 24
   B. $37 - 13$
   C. $30 - 13 = 17$
   D. $37 - 10 - 3 = 24$

5. There are 172 third graders and 128 fourth graders students on the playground. What is the total number of students on the playground? Which of the following option used place value addition?

   A. $172 + 128 = 300$
   B. $100 + 72 + 100 + 28 = 300$
   C. $172 + 100 + 28 = 300$
   D. $100 + 100 = 200 : 70 + 20 = 90 :$
      $2 + 8 = 10$: Total $= 300$

3.4B Round to the nearest 10 or 100 or use compatible numbers to estimate solutions to addition and subtraction problems.

1. What is 92 rounded to the nearest ten? A. 100 B. 90 C. 80 D. 9	2. What is 871 rounded to the nearest hundred? A. 900 B. 800 C. 850 D. 1000
3. Which addition problem has a sum of about 90? A. $45 + 36$ B. $53 + 39$ C. $51 + 48$ D. $63 + 36$	4. Which addition problem has a sum of about 90? A. $45 + 36$ B. $53 + 39$ C. $51 + 48$ D. $63 + 36$
5. A number has digits 6 and 8. To the nearest ten the number rounds to 70. What is the number? A. 60 B. 80 C. 86 D. 68	

PROBLEM SET 30

> 3.4B Round to the nearest 10 or 100 or use compatible numbers to estimate solutions to addition and subtraction problems

1. A number has digits 2, 1 and 8. To the nearest hundred the number rounds to 200. What is the number?

   A. 128
   B. 812
   C. 218
   D. 281

2. What is $9.20 rounded to the nearest dollar?

   A. 9
   B. 10
   C. 92
   D. 920

3. Which sign makes the statement true?

   $$81 - 12 \ \boxed{} \ 88 - 21$$

   A. <
   B. >
   C. =
   D. None of these

4. Which addition problem has a sum of about 900?

   A. 452 + 428
   B. 208 + 812
   C. 452 + 218
   D. 503 + 281

5. Which addition problem has a sum of about 600?

   A. 362 + 428
   B. 208 + 412
   C. 472 + 318
   D. 543 + 181

3.4D Determine the total number of objects when equally sized groups of objects are combined or arranged in arrays up to 10 by 10.

1. Sam got some blue marbles and some red marbles. He arranged the marbles in the array shown below. Write an addition sentence to find the total number of marbles based on the picture (for example, $2 + 1 = 3$).

A. $16 + 2$
B. $16 + 4$
C. $14 + 4$
D. $14 + 2$

2. A juice counter serves orange juice in orange glass and water melon juice in red glass. The shop keeper arranged the glasses as shown in the picture below. Find the total number of glasses.

Write an addition sentence based on the picture (for example, $2 + 1 = 3$).

A. $20 + 2$
B. $27 + 2$
C. $20 + 6$
D. $30 + 2$

3. Rebecca has eight pet rabbits. Each rabbit eats 3 apples every day. Find the total number of apples eaten by the rabbits in three days. Write a multiplication sentence based on the picture (for example, $2 \times 1 = 2$).

A. 7×3
B. $8 + 3$
C. 8×3
D. 8×4

4. Maya painted some kettles in blue and red colors. Write an addition sentence based on the picture below to find the total number of kettles Maya painted(for example, $2 + 1 = 3$).

A. $30 + 6$
B. $40 + 4$
C. $40 + 6$
D. $38 + 6$

5. Melissa separated her counters into 6 piles. Each pile contain 7 counters. How many total counters did Melissa have? Write a multiplication sentence based on the picture (for example, $2 \times 1 = 2$).

A. 6×7
B. $6 + 7$
C. 7×5
D. 8×6

PROBLEM SET 32

3.4D. Determine the total number of objects when equally sized groups of objects are combined or arranged in arrays up to 10 by 10.

1. Dino has a fun fair in his school. He displayed his blue and green marble in the array shown below. The kids were asked to tell the total number of marbles using an addition sentence based on the picture (for example, $2 + 1 = 3$).

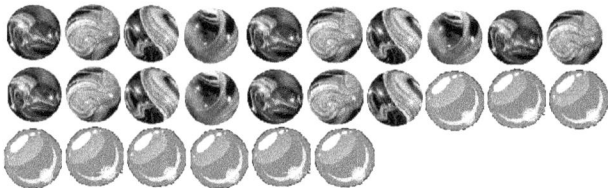

A. $20 + 6$
B. $17 + 9$
C. $30 + 6$
D. $17 + 6$

2. Sara collected some pink flowers and some orange flowers from her garden and arranged the flowers in the array shown below. Now she wanted to know how many flowers are there in total. Write an addition sentence based on the picture (for example, $2 + 1 = 3$).

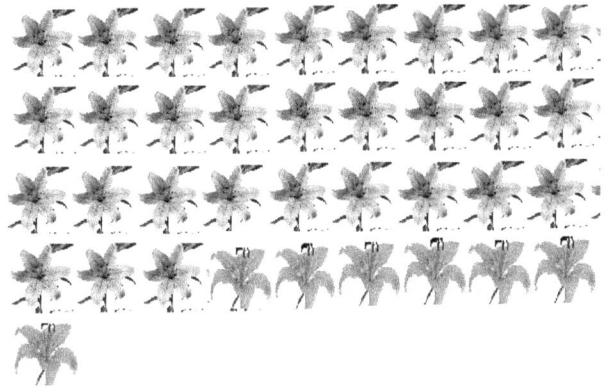

A. $40 + 1$
B. $30 + 1$
C. $20 + 7$
D. $30 + 7$

3. Karl takes three minutes to iron a shirt and five minutes to iron a trouser. The blue blocks represents the number of shirts and yellow blocks represents number of trousers. Write an addition sentence based on the picture below to find the total number of clothes Karl ironed (for example, 2 + 1 = 3).

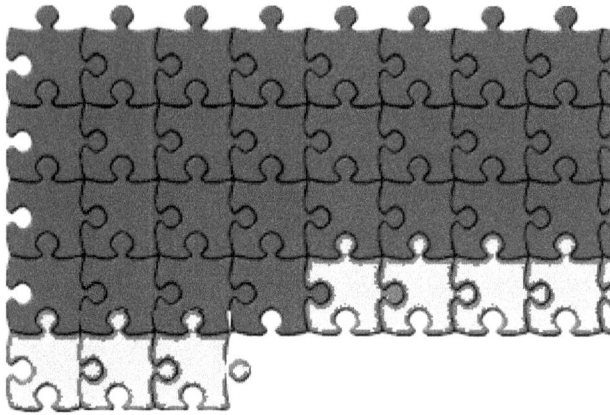

A. 32 + 3   B. va30 + 7
C. 40 + 7   D. 28 + 7

4. Mom baked two types of cookies for Lara's birthday. She arranged the cookies in an array shown below. Write an addition sentence based on the picture below to find the total number of cookies Mom baked (for example, 2 + 1 = 3).

A. 40 + 2   B. 30 + 7
C. 31 + 7   D. 40 + 7

5. Arya has some red hot wheels and some blue hot wheels. He arranged his hot wheels in an array shown below. Find the total number of hot wheels Arya has. Write an addition sentence based on the picture (for example, 2 + 1 = 3).

A. 40 + 6   B. 31 + 7
C. 30 + 7   D. 30 + 6

PROBLEM SET 33

3.4E *Represent multiplication facts by using a variety of approaches such as repeated addition, equal-sized groups, arrays are models, equal jumps on a number line, and skip counting.*

1. How many cubes are there? Count by fives.

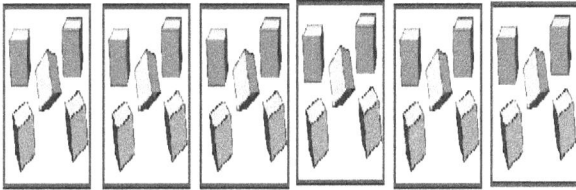

A. 6   B. 25
C. 30   D. 20

2. How many cherries are there? Count by tens.

A. 60   B. 70
C. 50   D. 7

3. Julia reads 3 pages of a book every day. Find the total number of pages she read in 4 days using equal jumps on the number line below.

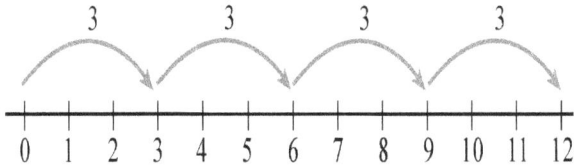

A. 3   B. 4
C. 9   D. 12

4. This shape is made out of unit squares. What is the area?

A. 3   B. 9
C. 2   D. 1

5. Which of the following repeated addition is equal to 7×4?

A. 7
B. $7 + 7 + 7$
C. $7 + 7 + 7 + 7$
D. $7 + 7 + 7 + 7 + 7 + 7$

3.4E Represent multiplication facts by using a variety of approaches such as repeated addition, equal-sized groups, arrays are models, equal jumps on a number line, and skip counting.

1. Jack began at 51. He skip-counted until he got to 65. Which number did he use for skip counting?

A. 3
B. 4
C. 5
D. 7

2. Complete the multiplication sentence that describes the model.

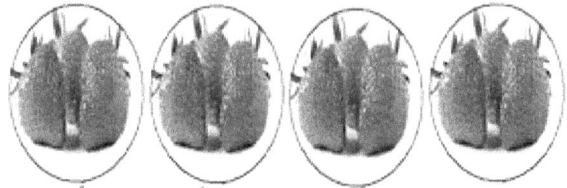

6 X ☐ = 24

A. 3   B. 4
C. 6   D. 5

3. Complete the multiplication sentence that describes the model.

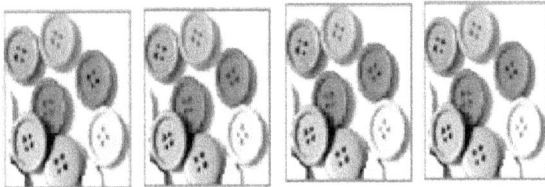

7 X ☐ = 28

A. 4   B. 7
C. 6   D. 5

4. Which of the following option represents the above array?

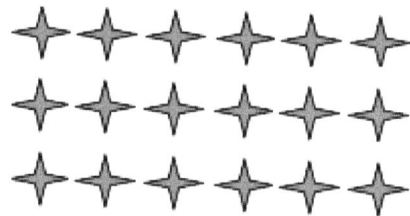

A. 6
B. 6 + 6
C. 3 × 3
D. 6 + 6 + 6

5. Maya started at 45. She skip-counted until she reached 95. She has been counting by which number?

A. 10   B. 9
C. 6   D. 42

PROBLEM SET 35

3.4F *Recall facts to multiply up to 10 by 10 with automaticity and recall the corresponding division facts*	

1. $7 \times 6 =$ A. 13 B. 32 C. 56 D. 42	**2.** $42 \div 7 =$ A. 6 B. 8 C. 7 D. 35
3. If it takes Cooper 3 minute to clean a table, how many tables could he clean in 12 minutes? A. 4 B. 36 C. 9 D. 15	**4.** Sarah has 6 apples. She cuts apples in 8 slices. How many apple slices did Sarah make? A. 42 B. 14 C. 48 D. 2
5. Fill the missing number: 8 X ☐ = 56 A. 6 B. 5 C. 7 D. 9	

3.4F Recall facts to multiply up to 10 by 10 with automaticity and recall the corresponding division facts

---

1. Fill the missing number:

$$8 \times \boxed{} = 56$$

A. 6
B. 5
C. 7
D. 9

2. Maria's sticker collection fills 5 pages in her sticker book. There are 8 stickers on each page. How many stickers are in Maria's collection?

A. 40
B. 13
C. 3
D. 30

---

3. Maria's sticker collection fills 5 pages in her sticker book. There are 8 stickers on each page. How many stickers are in Maria's collection?

A. 40
B. 13
C. 3
D. 30

4. Charles used 60 stamps to mail 6 letters. He used the same number of stamps on each letter. Find the number of stamps did Charles put on each letter?

A. 66
B. 10
C. 54
D. 6

---

5. A bakery shop put 5 bagels in each basket. If Chelsey and her friends want 30 bagels, how many baskets should they buy?

A. 5
B. 25
C. 6
D. 10

PROBLEM SET 37

> 3.4G Use strategies and algorithms, including the standard algorithm, to multiply a two-digit number by a one-digit number. Strategies may include mental math, partial products, and the commutative, associative, and distributive properties.

1. Sana wants to buy four chairs for her house. What is the cost of buying four chairs for $48 each? (Use standard algorithm to multiply)

   A. $40 \times 4 + \$8 \times 4 = 192$
   B. $\$48 \times 4 = \$192$
   C. $\$40 \times 4 + \$5 \times 4 + \$3 \times 4 = 192$
   D. $\$45 \times 4 = \$192$

2. Ria bought 6 boxes of pens. There were 52 pens in each box. How many pens did Ria buy? (Use standard algorithm to multiply)

   A. $52 \times 6 = 312$
   B. $50 \times 6 + 2 \times 6 = 312$
   C. $52 \times 5 = 260$
   D. $10 \times 6 + 20 \times 6 + 30 \times 6 + 2 \times 6 = 312$

3. Mr. Goggins set up 44 rows of chairs in the gymnasium. If each row had 6 chairs, how many chairs did Mr. Goggins set up? Which of the following option uses partial product?

   A. $44 \times 6 = 264$
   B. $44 \times 5 + 44 \times 1 = 264$
   C. $30 \times 4 + 14 \times 4 = 264$
   D. $40 \times 6 + 4 \times 6 = 264$

4. Bipasa's mother gave her 4 packages of stickers. There were 213 stickers in each package. How many stickers did Bipasa's mother give her in all? Which of the following option uses partial product?

   A. $213 \times 4 = 852$
   B. $210 \times 4 = 840$
   C. $200 \times 4 + 10 \times 4 + 3 \times 4 = 852$
   D. $2 \times 4 + 1 \times 4 + 3 \times 4 = 24$

5. Sam and Dan set up nine rows of seats in the school auditorium, with 14 seats in each row. How many seats are there in total? Which of the following option shows the property of Cummutative law to achieve the answer?

   A. $10 \times 9 + 4 \times 9 = 131$
   B. $10 + 4 \times 9 = 131$
   C. $9 \times 14 = 14 \times 9 = 131$
   D. $14 \times 9 = 131$

PROBLEM SET 38

3.4G Use strategies and algorithms, including the standard algorithm, to multiply a two-digit number by a one-digit number. Strategies may include mental math, partial products, and the commutative, associative, and distributive properties.

1. The following blocks shows which property of multiplication?

$3 \times (2+4)$ $3 \times 2 + 3 \times 4$

A. Commutative
B. Distributive
C. Associative
D. None of these

2. The capacity of a drum is 70 liters of milk. How much milk can be collected in 7 drums of such capacity? (Calculate mentally and answer)

A. 49
B. 490
C. 420
D. 560

3. According to Associative law $8 \times (6 \times 7)$ is also equal to:

A. $8 \times 6 + 7$
B. $(8 \times 6) \times 7$
C. $8 + 6 \times 7$
D. $8 \times 7 + 6$

4. Ms. Faria writes the following number sentence on the board:

$$600 \times \boxed{} = 0$$

Which number would go into the box?

A. 0
B. 1
C. 2
D. 3

5. There are 60 minutes in an hour. How many minutes are there in a day of 24 hours?

A. 1200
B. 1441
C. 1440
D. 1240

PROBLEM SET 39

3.4H Determine the number of objects in each group when a set of objects is partitioned into equal shares or a set of objects is shared equally.

1. An airplane can hold 60 passengers. If there are 12 rows of seats on the airplane, how many seats are in each row?

A. 4
B. 6
C. 5
D. 8

2. A farmer is filling baskets of oranges. The farmer has 36 oranges and 9 baskets. If he divides them equally, how many oranges will he put in each basket?

A. 8
B. 6
C. 5
D. 4

3. Helen went bird watching and took 8 pictures of each bird she saw. If Helen took a total of 32 pictures, how many different birds did she see?

A. 4
B. 6
C. 5
D. 8

4. Lisa has 18 markers. Her mother gives her three boxes and asks her to put an equal number of markers in each box. How many markers Lisa should fill in each box?

A. 4
B. 6
C. 5
D. 8

5. Sam has 48 red balloons. He wants to give his eight friends the same number of red balloons, how many will each friend get?

A. 4
B. 5
C. 6
D. 8

PROBLEM SET 40

> 3.4H Determine the number of objects in each group when a set of objects is partitioned into equal shares or a set of objects is shared equally.

1. At a certain restaurant, each table seats 8 people. How many tables will a group of 56 people need?

A. 4
B. 7
C. 6
D. 8

2. A bakery shop sold 42 bagels last week. How many bagels on average were sold each day?

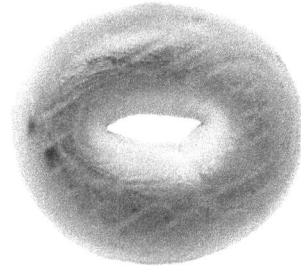

A. 4
B. 5
C. 7
D. 6

3. A group of 6 girls collected a total of 24 cans for recycling. If they each collected the same amount, how many cans did each girl collect?

A. 4
B. 5
C. 7
D. 6

4. Tina goes out to lunch with Lara and Nancy. The total bill came to 21 dollars. They decided to equally split up the bill, how much will each person have to pay?

A. 4
B. 5
C. 6
D. 7

5. Jara was at the beach for four days with her parents and found 28 seashells. She plans to give all of her seashells equally to her four friends. How many seashells will each friend get?

A. 4

B. 5

C. 7

D. 6

PROBLEM SET 41

3.4J. Determine a quotient using the relationship between multiplication and division.

When a number is multiplied and divided by the same number, the result is the original number.

---

1. Kate runs 4 kilometers every day. How many days will it take her to run 24 kilometers?

   A. 4
   B. 5
   C. 6
   D. 7

2. What will be the equivalent multiplication of

   $60 \div 5 = 12$?

   A. $60 \times 5 = 300$
   B. $5 \times 12 = 60$
   C. $12 \times 60 = 720$
   D. $60 \times 12 \times 5$

3. Fill in the blank to make each equation true.

   $$12 \div 3 \times _____ = 12$$

   A. 5
   B. 4
   C. 3
   D. 2

4. The nursery can put 8 plants in each pot. If they need to plant 48 plants, how many pots will they need to use?

   A. 8
   B. 7
   C. 6
   D. 5

5. Type a multiplication fact of

   $$54 \div 6 = 9$$

   A. $6 \times 9 = 54$
   B. $54 \times 6 \times 9$
   C. $54 \div 6 \times 9$
   D. $9 \div 6 \times 54$

PROBLEM SET 42

3.4J. Determine a quotient using the relationship between multiplication and division.

When a number is multiplied and divided by the same number, the result is the original number.

1. A small scissor costs $18. Another, much better one, is four times as expensive. Find the cost of the more expensive scissor.

A. $36
B. $16
C. $54
D. $72

2. What will be the equivalent multiplication of

$$56 \div 8 = 7?$$

A. $56 \times 8 = 448$
B. $56 \times 7 = 392$
C. $56 \times 8 \times 7$
D. $8 \times 7 = 56$

3. What will be the equivalent multiplication of $56 \div 8 = 7$?

A. $56 \times 8 = 448$
B. $56 \times 7 = 392$
C. $56 \times 8 \times 7$
D. $8 \times 7 = 56$

4. What will be the equivalent multiplication of $56 \div 8 = 7$?

A. $56 \times 8 = 448$
B. $56 \times 7 = 392$
C. $56 \times 8 \times 7$
D. $8 \times 7 = 56$

5. For a relay race, each team needs 9 people. If 54 people participate in the race, how many teams will there be?

A. 6
B. 5
C. 7
D. 4

3.4K Solve one-step and two-step problems involving multiplication and division within 100 using strategies based on objects; pictorial models, including arrays, area models, and equal groups; properties of operations; or recall of facts.

1. Emma collects lady bugs. She arranges them in 6 rows of 8. Which of the following represents Emma's array to show how many lady bugs she has all together. Then, write a multiplication equation to describe the array.

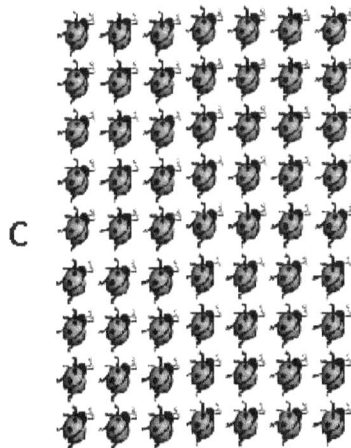

A

B

C

D. None of these

2. Mom bought 7 boxes of cookies. There were 12 cookies in each box. How many cookies did mom buy?

A. 82
B. 85
C. 84
D. 72

3. Which of the following multiplication sentence describes the model?

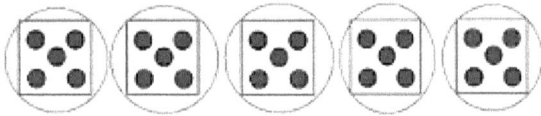

A. $5 + 5$ 10
B. $5 \times 4 = 20$
C. $5 \times 5 = 25$
D. $5 \times 6 = 30$

4. Which of the following multiplication sentence describes the model?

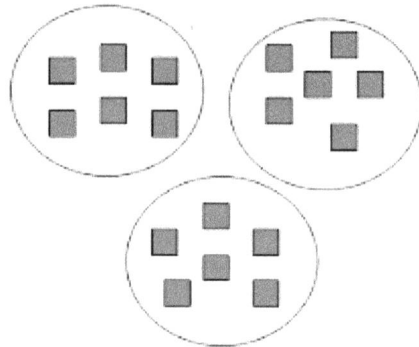

A. $2 \times 6 = 12$
B. $3 \times 5 = 15$
C. $3 \times 4 = 12$
D. $3 \times 6 = 18$

5. Keith modeled 4×6 using the following models. Which models are accurate representations of the multiplication of these two factors?

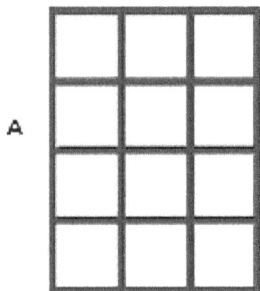

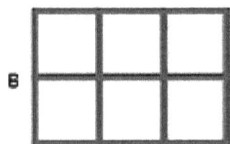

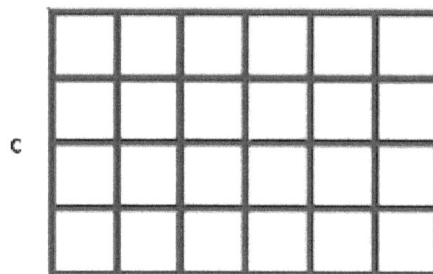

A

B

C

D. None of these

3.4K Solve one-step and two-step problems involving multiplication and division within 100 using strategies based on objects; pictorial models, including arrays, area models, and equal groups; properties of operations; or recall of facts.

1. John is planning a party at his house. He arranged the chairs for his friend in the following area model. Which of the following option represents the correct number?

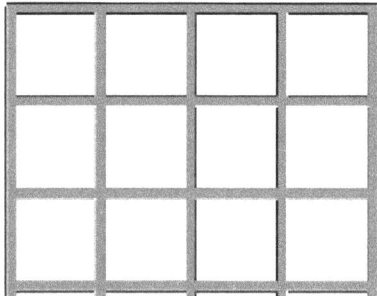

   A. $3 \times 4 = 12$
   B. $4 \times 4 = 16$
   C. $3 \times 3 = 9$
   D. $3 \times 5 = 15$

2. Suzain is making bows to decorate for her birthday party. She bought 108 meters of ribbon, and it takes 9 meters of ribbon to make each bow. How many bows can Suzain make?

   A. 9
   B. 10
   C. 11
   D. 12

3. Tiara wants to buy 81 soft toys for return gift in her birthday party. If there are 9 soft toys in each pack, how many packs of cat toys should Tiara buy?

   A. 9
   B. 10
   C. 8
   D. 7

4. Children sit in 3 rows of 8 on the carpet for quiz time. Brian says, "We make 3 equal groups." Jada says, "We make 8 equal groups." Who is correct?

   A. Brian
   B. Jada
   C. Both are correct
   D. Both are wrong

5. Charlie organizes cans of food into an array. He thinks, "My cans show 7×3!" His brother came and arranges the cans in different array but the total number was same. Which option can be true for both?

A. $7 \times 3 = 21$

B. $7 \times 3 = 7 + 3$

C. $3 \times 7 = 3 + 7$

D. $7 \times 3 = 3 \times 7$

PROBLEM SET 45

> 3.5A represent one- and two-step problems involving addition and subtraction of whole numbers to 1,000 using pictorial models, number lines, and equations.

1. Write a subtraction sentence based on the picture (for example, $3 - 1 = 2$).

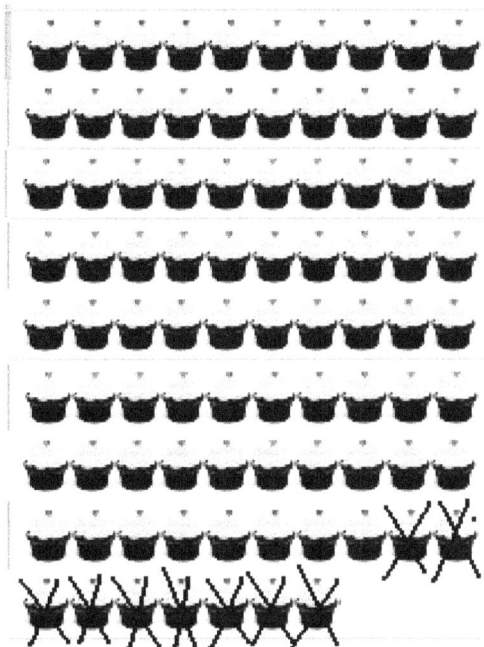

A. $87 - 7 = 80$
B. $90 - 7 = 83$
C. $87 - 9 = 78$
D. $87 - 10 = 77$

2. Sally found 72 seashells but 6 were broken. How many unbroken seashells did Sally find? Write a subtraction sentence based on the picture (for example, $3 - 1 = 2$).

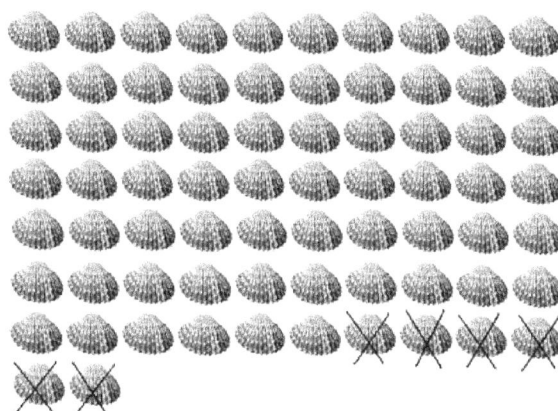

A. $70 - 6 = 64$
B. $72 - 6 = 66$
C. $88 - 2 = 86$
D. $62 - 6 = 54$

3. Rebecca collected some red apples and some green apples from her farm. Using the picture below write the total number of red and green apples (1 apple = 10)

A. 28 + 6
B. 300 + 40
C. 280 + 60
D. 280 + 40

4. Jara ordered some popsicles for her party. When the popsicles was delivered at her home she wanted to make sure that is it correct number or not? Help her to count the total number of popsicles.

A. 76
B. 60
C. 66
D. 56

5. The vegetable shop has 912 kg potato. They also have 41 kg onion. Overall, how many kg do they have?

A. 952
B. 953
C. 951
D. 956

3.5A represent one- and two-step problems involving addition and subtraction of whole numbers to 1,000 using pictorial models, number lines, and equations.

---

1. Write a suntraction sentence based on the number line below (for example, $3 - 1 = 2$).

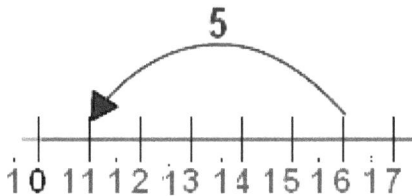

$$5$$

10 11 12 13 14 15 16 17

A. $11 + 5 = 16$
B. $11 + 6 = 17$
C. $16 - 6 = 10$
D. $16 - 5 = 11$

2. Write an addition sentence based on the number line below (for example, $3 + 1 = 4$).

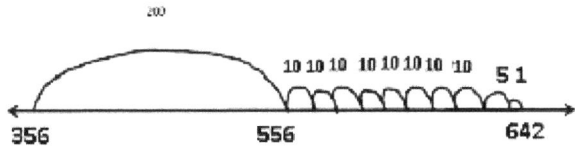

200

10 10 10 10 10 10 10 10   5 1

356   556   642

A. $356 + 642 = 998$
B. $356 + 42 = 798$
C. $356 + 556 = 912$
D. $356 + 286 = 642$

---

3. Ivana has 68 blue blocks. When she mixes them with her red blocks, there are 82 blocks in all. Which equation, when solved, will show how many red blocks Ivana has?

A. $68 + r = 82$
B. $68 \times r = 82$
C. $68 - r = 82$
D. $68 + 82 = r$

4. Josh and Patrick collected seashells on the beach. Josh found 17 shells. When Josh and Patrick put all of their shells together, they had 56 shells. Which equation, when solved, will show how many shells Patrick found?

A. $56 + 17 = t$
B. $56 + t = 17$
C. $17 + t = 56$
D. $56 \times 17 = t$

5. Josh and Patrick collected seashells on the beach. Josh found 17 shells. When Josh and Patrick put all of their shells together, they had 56 shells. Which equation, when solved, will show how many shells Patrick found?

A. $56 + 17 = t$

B. $56 + t = 17$

C. $17 + t = 56$

D. $56 \times 17 = t$

PROBLEM SET 47

3.5B *Represent and solve one- and two-step multiplication and division problems within 100 using arrays, strip diagrams, and equations.*

---

1. Which option is true about the array below?

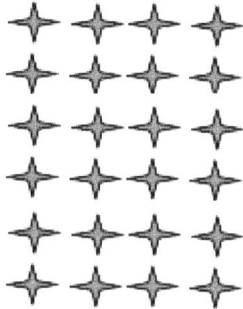

   A. $4 \times 6 = 24$
   B. $4 + 4 + 4 + 4 + 4 + 4 = 24$
   C. $6 \times 4 = 24$
   D. $6 + 6 + 6 + 6 = 24$

2. Which option is true about the array below?

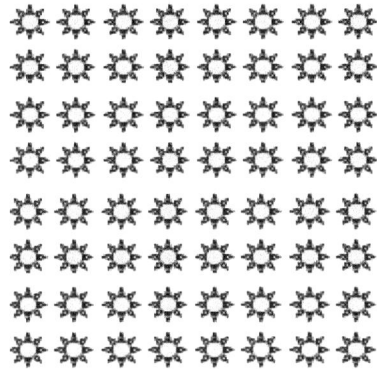

   A. $8 \times 6 = 48$
   B. $8 \times 8 = 64$
   C. $8 + 8 = 16$
   D. $8 + 8 + 8 + 8 + 8 + 8 + 8 + 8 = 64$

---

3. Jenny has 4 pencils in her zip pouch. Pamella has 3 times more pencils than Jenny. How many total number of pencils? Which strip diagram demonstrates the correct answer?

A

| 4 | 4 | 4 | 4 | = 16 |

B

| 4 | 4 | 4 | = 12 |

C

| 4 | 4 | 3 | = 11 |

   D.   None of these

4. Two bunnies sat on the grass. Four more bunnies hopped there. How many bunnies are on the grass now? Which strip diagram demonstrates the correct answer?

A

| 2 | 3 | = 5 |

B

| 2 | 4 | = 6 |

C

| 2 | 2 | = 4 |

   D.   None of these

5. Anna goes out to lunch with Lara and Ria. The total bill came to 27 dollars. They decided to equally split up the bill, how much will each person have to pay?

A. 9
B. 8
C. 7
D. 6

PROBLEM SET 48

> 3.5B *Represent and solve one- and two-step multiplication and division problems within 100 using arrays, strip diagrams, and equations.*

1. Anna goes out to lunch with Lara and Ria. The total bill came to 27 dollars. They decided to equally split up the bill, how much will each person have to pay?

   A. 9
   B. 8
   C. 7
   D. 6

2. Helen bought a box of pushpins. She put 7 pushpins on the bulletin board and had 45 left. Which equation, when solved, will tell how many pushpins were in the box?

   A. $52 - p = 45$
   B. $45 + p = 52$
   C. $p - 7 = 45$
   D. $45 + p = 7$

3. Alan bought 8 gummy worms at the candy store. His friend Fedrick also bought some gummy worms. When they counted all of them together, Alan and Fedrick had 60 gummy worms. Which equation, when solved, will show how many gummy worms Fedrick bought?

   A. $8 + w = 60$
   B. $8 - 60 = w$
   C. $8 - w = 60$
   D. $60 + 8 = w$

4. A party supply store ordered paper cups. Each package contains 5 stacks of cups, and there are 5 cups in each stack. How many paper cups are there in 5 packages?

   A. 55
   B. 45
   C. 25
   D. 125

5. A pizza shop charges $4 for a slice of pizza. They cut each whole pizza into 5 slices. How much money will the pizza shop make if they sell 3 pizza?

   A. 50
   B. 60
   C. 20
   D. 30

> *3.5C Describe a multiplication expression as a comparison such as 3 × 24 represents 3 times as much as 24.*

---

1. Meera baked 4 batches of cookies. Each batch contained 72 cookies. How many cookies did Meera bake?

A. 278
B. 298
C. 288
D. 388

2. There are 7 boxes of pencils in the supply closet. Each box contains 52 pencils. How many pencils are there in all?

A. 364
B. 264
C. 284
D. 354

---

3. Aliya has 4 types of 5 hair clips each. She wants a multiplication expression which will represent the total number of her hair clips.

A. 4 × 5 = 20
B. 5 × 4 = 20
C. 4 times as much as 20
D. All of the above

4. The Laila family has six members. Each member has two small towels and a bath towel. How many towels hang in the bathroom?

A. 18
B. 16
C. 17
D. 14

---

5. The plane goes 700 miles an hour. The car goes 50 miles an hour. How many times faster than the car is the plane?

A. 18
B. 16
C. 17
D. 14

PROBLEM SET 50

3.5C Describe a multiplication expression as a comparison such as 3 × 24 represents 3 times as much as 24.

---

1. Sonit has 9 video games. Bent has 63 video games. How many times more video games does Bent have than Sonit?

A. 8
B. 9
C. 7
D. 6

2. Karla is canning oranges. If each jar holds 9 oranges and Karla has 81 oranges, how many jars will he need?

A. 8
B. 9
C. 7
D. 6

---

3. If Alan swims exactly 15 kilometres every week, how many weeks will it take Alan to swim 90 kilometres?

A. 8
B. 7
C. 5
D. 6

4. Charles and Vicky both collect stickers. Vicky has six times as many stickers as Charles. If Vicky has 24 stickers, how many stickers does Charles have?

A. 244
B. 144
C. 142
D. 134

---

5. Charles and Vicky both collect stickers. Vicky has six times as many stickers as Charles. If Vicky has 24 stickers, how many stickers does Charles have?

A. 244
B. 144
C. 142
D. 134

3.5D Determine the unknown whole number in a multiplication or division equation relating three whole numbers when the unknown is either a missing factor or product.

1. In the back of the store, Mr. Sherman packs 56 bell peppers equally into 8 bags. How many bell peppers are in each bag?

A. 5
B. 6
C. 7
D. 8

2. A mint factory puts 9 mints in each box. How many mints will the factory need to fill 12 boxes?

A. 92
B. 108
C. 96
D. 104

3. Stacey bought 6 bags of candy. There were 9 pieces of candy in each bag. How many pieces of candy did Stacey buy?

A. 54
B. 52
C. 60
D. 45

4. Each day, Faria rides her bicycle for 2 kilometer. How many days will it take Faria to ride 12 kilometers?

A. 5
B. 6
C. 7
D. 8

5. Julia has 80 puppies. She has 10 times as many puppies as her brother Josheph. Which equation will help us find how many puppies Josheph has?

A. $80 \div 10 = 8$
B. $8 \times 10 = 80$
C. $80 - 8 = 72$
D. $80 - 10 = 70$

> 3.5D Determine the unknown whole number in a multiplication or division equation relating three whole numbers when the unknown is either a missing factor or product.

1. Sofia uses 3 lemons to make 1 pitcher of lemonade. He makes 7 pitchers. How many lemons does she use all together?

   A. 22
   B. 18
   C. 21
   D. 20

2. Jasmine has 28 wheels to make toy cars. She uses 4 wheels for each car. How many toy cars she can make?

   A. 5
   B. 6
   C. 7
   D. 8

3. Ms. Rose has 7 boxes of marker. Each box has 12 pieces of markers. How many pieces of markers does the Ms. Rose have?

   A. 80
   B. 84
   C. 72
   D. 85

4. Ms. Kathy has 54 stickers. She puts 6 stickers on each homework paper and has no more left. How many homework papers does she have?

   A. 8
   B. 9
   C. 10
   D. 11

5. Jasmine puts 28 books away. She puts an equal number of books on 4 shelves. How many books are on each shelf?

   A. 8
   B. 9
   C. 10
   D. 7

3.5E

1. Maria bought some muffins. They came in 13 identical boxes. Each box had 4 muffins. Which equation, when solved, will tell how many muffins Maria bought in all?

A. $x - 13 = 4$
B. $x \div 13 = 4$
C. $x + 13 = 4$
D. $x \div 13 = 52$

2. Maria bought some muffins. They came in 13 identical boxes. Each box had 4 muffins. Which equation, when solved, will tell how many muffins Maria bought in all?

A. $x - 13 = 4$
B. $x \div 13 = 4$
C. $x + 13 = 4$
D. $x \div 13 = 52$

3. What is the rule for this input/output table?

In	Out
8	4
10	5
12	6

A. $\div 1$
B. $\div 2$
C. $\div 3$
D. $\div 4$

4. What is the rule for this input/output table?

In	Out
4	1
8	2
12	3

A. $\div 1$
B. $\div 2$
C. $\div 3$
D. $\div 4$

5. What is the rule for this input/output table?

In	Out
6	12
7	14
8	16

A. $\times 1$
B. $\times 2$
C. $\times 3$
D. $\times 4$

3.5E

1. What is the rule for this input/output table?

In	Out
8	24
9	27
10	30

A. x 1
B. x 2
C. x 3
D. x 4

2. Sofaya bought some clips. She used 9 of the clips and had 21 clips left. How many clips did she buy?

A. $b - 9 = 21$
B. $b + 9 = 21$
C. $21 \div 9 = b$
D. $9 \times b = 21$

3. What is the rule for this input/output table?

In	Out
12	4
15	5
18	6

A. ÷ 1
B. ÷ 2
C. ÷ 3
D. ÷ 4

4. Neil bought some stamps. He used 23 of the stamps and had 49 stamps left. How many stamps did he buy?

A. $b - 23 = 49$
B. $b + 23 = 49$
C. $49 \div 23 = b$
D. $17 \times b = 49$

5. Samolina bought some boxes of cupcakes. There were 6 cupcakes in each box, and Samolina bought 60 donuts in all. Which equation, when solved, will tell how many boxes of cupcakes Samolina bought?

A. $60 \times 6 = m$
B. $m + 6 = 60$
C. $m \times 6 = 60$
D. $m \div 6 = 60$

REPORTING CATEGORY 3 (READINESS)
GEOMETRY & MEASUREMENT

PROBLEM SET 55

3.6A classify and sort two- and three-dimensional figures, including cones, cylinders, spheres, triangular and rectangular prisms, and cubes, based on attributes using formal geometric language.

1. Sarah made some shapes and confused about the shapes. She wanted to know which shape is square?

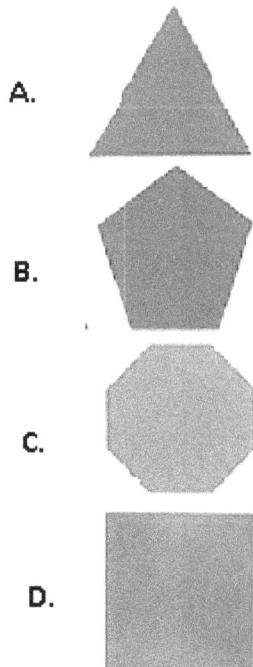

A.

B.

C.

D.

2. Laila made a 3-dimensional figure out of cardboard. The figure had a round base. Which figure could Laila have made?

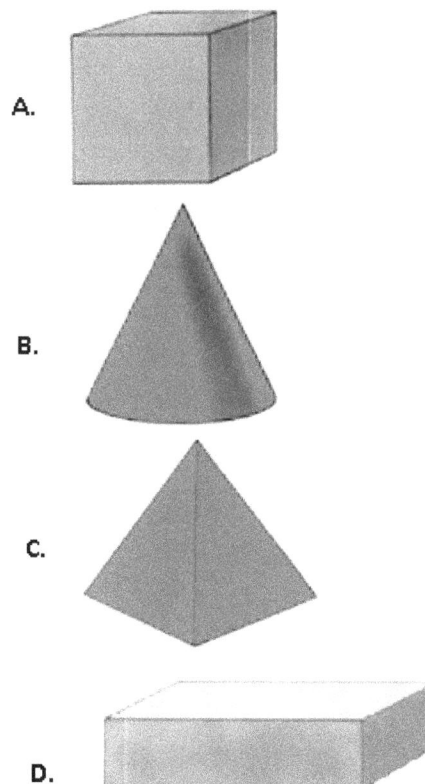

A.

B.

C.

D.

3. Which of these is a triangular prism?

A.

B.

C.

D.

4. Josheph cut a shape out of a piece of construction paper. The shape had 3 equal angles. Which shape could Josheph have made?

A. Triangle

B. Octagon

C. Hexagon

D. Pentagon

5. Alex made some shapes and confused about the angles. Help Alex to know which shape has more angles?

A.

B.

C.

D.

PROBLEM SET 56

3.6A *classify and sort two- and three-dimensional figures, including cones, cylinders, spheres, triangular and rectangular prisms, and cubes, based on attributes using formal geometric language.*

1. Which of the following is a cylinder?

A.

B.

C.

D.

2. Which figure is this?

A. Polygon
B. Cone
C. Circle
D. Triangle

3. Alisha's younger sister drew a shape that had 6 sides. Alisha wants to help her. Which shape could she have drawn?

A. Hexagon
B. Triangle
C. Circle
D. Decagon

4. Alex made a 3-dimensional figure out of clay. The figure had 6 vertices. Which figure could Alex have made?

A. Triangular prism
B. Cube
C. Cone
D. Rectangular pyramid

5. Shaun made a 3-dimensional figure out of wood. The figure had a round shape, like a ball. Which figure could Shaun have made?

A. Triangular prism
B. Sphere
C. Rectangular pyramid
D. Cone

3.6B use attributes to recognize rhombuses, parallelograms, trapezoids, rectangles, and squares as examples of quadrilaterals and draw examples of quadrilaterals that do not belong to any of these subcategories.

1. Dora drew a shape that had 4 sides and 4 equal angles. Which shape could Dora have drawn?

A. **Hexagon**

B. **Pentagon**

C. **Octagon**

D. **Square**

2. Which of the following is NOT true?

A. A parallelogram has opposite sides Parallel and equal in length.

B. A square has opposite sides parallel. It's all sides are equal and all angles are right angles.

C. A rectangle is parallelogram with four equal sides and four right angles.

D. A trapezoid is four-sided polygon having exactly one pair of parallel sides.

3. Sujain cut a shape out of a piece of construction paper. The shape is four-sided closed figure. The opposite sides are equal and parallel. Which shape could Sujain have made?

A. **Triangle**

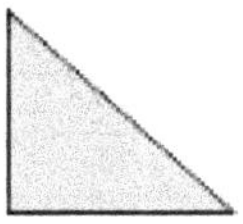

B. **Parallelogram**

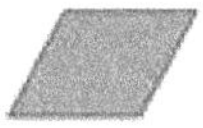

C. **Circle**

D. **Trapezoid**

4. Ben drew a shape that had 4 sides. The opposite sides are equal and parallel but angles are not right angle. Which shape could Ben have drawn?

A. **Triangle**

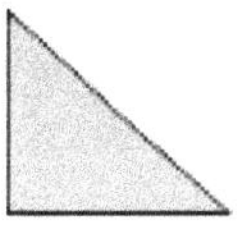

B. **Parallelogram**

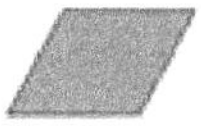

C. **Circle**

D. **Rectangle**

5. Nora painted a shape that had 4 sides but not all are equal. Which shape could Nora have painted?

A. **Triangle**

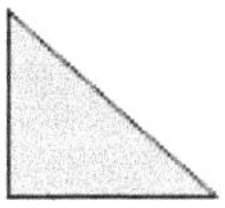

B. **Trapezoid**

C. **Circle**

D. **Octagon**

PROBLEM SET 58

> *3.6B use attributes to recognize rhombuses, parallelograms, trapezoids, rectangles, and squares as examples of quadrilaterals and draw examples of quadrilaterals that do not belong to any of these subcategories.*

1. Which of the following Quadrilateral does not have all for angles as right angles?

A. Parallelogram
B. Rectangle
C. Square
D. All of above

2. Which figure is quadrilateral?

A.
C.
B.
D.

3. Jeanette says her shape is quadrilateral in which the sides can be grouped into two pairs of adjacent equal-length sides. Which shape is this?

A. Rectangle   B. Square
C. Parallelogram   D. Kite

4. Which of the following is NOT correct?

A. A rectangle has all opposite sides **are equal.**
B. A square has 4 sides and 4 angles.
C. A triangle has 5 sides and 5 angles.
D. All points of a circle are of same distance.

5. Mark painted a shape which is a four sided closed figure. The opposite sides are equal and parallel. Its each angle is 90⁰. Which is the figure?

A. Triangle   B. Trapezoid
C. Rectangle   D. Pentagon

PROBLEM SET 59

3.6C determine the area of rectangles with whole number side lengths in problems using multiplication related to the number of rows times the number of unit squares in each row.

1. A square bathroom tile has sides that are 7 inches long. What is the tile's area?

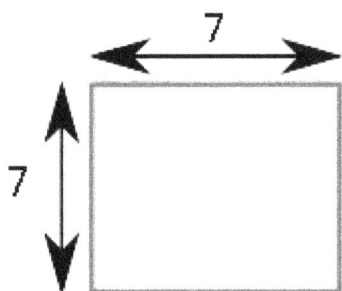

7

7

A. 42   B. 35
C. 49   D. 44

2. The football team plays at a stadium with dimensions of 20 feet × 30 feet of seating for spectators. Find the total area of the football stadium's spectator area?

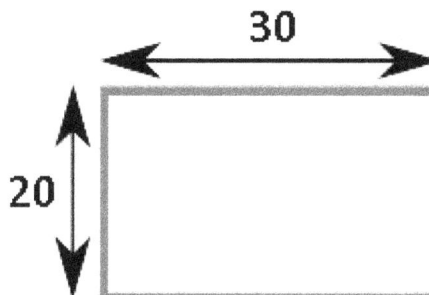

30

20

A. 50 feet   B. 500 feet
C. 60 feet   D. 600 feet

3. Mika bought a piece of land. The dimension of the land is 50 feet × 40 feet. Calculate the total area of the piece of land.

A. 2000 feet
B. 500 feet
C. 200 feet
D. 90 feet

4. Paula runs around a square park of side 75 feet. Laila runs around a rectangular park with length 60 feet and breadth 45 feet Who covers less distance?

A. Paula
B. Laila
C. Both covers same distance
D. None of above

5. A computer lab measures 60 feet × 35 feet. What is the area of computer lab?

A. 6000 feet
B. 1800 feet
C. 2100 feet
D. 6500 feet

3.6C determine the area of rectangles with whole number side lengths in problems using multiplication related to the number of rows times the number of unit squares in each row.

1. Ryan purchases a floor carpet for her room that is 9 feet × 8 feet. How much area is occupied by the carpet?

   A. 17 feet
   B. 72 feet
   C. 64 feet
   D. 81 feet

2. A candy shop acquires 70 feet × 60 feet in a new space. Find the area of the new shopping area?

   A. 1300 feet
   B. 4200 feet
   C. 2100 feet
   D. 4900 feet

3. Mona plans to start a coffee shop. She requires a large space for her shop. The following areas are available for rent. Which area should she choose?

   A. 8 feet × 10 feet
   B. 9 feet × 14 feet
   C. 8 feet × 21 feet
   D. 15 feet × 12 feet

4. Alan plans to open a dance academy. He requires a large space for his academy. The following areas are available for rent. Which area should he choose?

   A. 11 feet × 9 feet
   B. 9 feet × 15 feet
   C. 8 feet × 21 feet
   D. 15 feet × 8 feet

5. Find the missing side length, when the area is 16 square units.

   6 | Area = 54 sq. unit

   A. 8
   B. 7
   C. 9
   D. 4

3.6D decompose composite figures formed by rectangles into non-overlapping rectangles to determine the area of the original figure using the additive property of area.

1. Sarah house has a lawn but it is not a proper rectangle. Find the area of her lawn which is shown below.

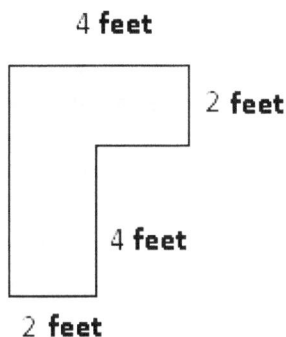

4 **feet**

2 **feet**

4 **feet**

2 **feet**

A. 8 sq. feet + 8 sq. feet = 16 sq. feet
B. 4 sq. feet + 4 sq. feet = 8 sq. feet
C. 4 sq. feet + 2 sq. feet = 6 sq. feet
D. $4 \times 2 \times 2 \times 4 = 64$ sq. feet

2. Laila has a nice living room. She wants to buy carpet for her living room. Find the area of the living room so that she can buy a proper size carpet.

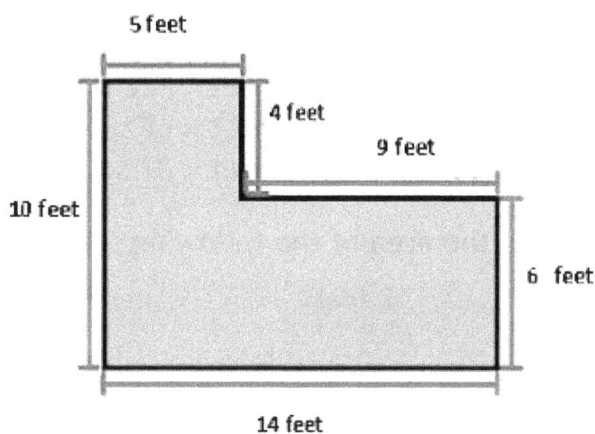

5 feet

4 feet

9 feet

10 feet

6 feet

14 feet

A. 10 feet × 5 feet + 4 feet x 9 feet + 6 feet × 14 feet = 188 sq. feet
B. 10 feet × 5 feet + 6 feet × 14 feet = 106 sq. feet
C. 10 feet × 5 feet + 9 feet × 5 feet = 95 sq. Feet
D. 10 feet × 5 feet + 9 feet × 6 feet = 104 sq. Feet

3. Alisha house has a backyard in the shape shown below. Find the area of her lawn which is shown below.

6 feet

10 feet

12 feet

5 feet

A. 18 sq. feet + 15 sq. feet = 33 sq. feet
B. 72 sq. feet + 50 sq. feet = 122 sq. feet
C. 18 sq. feet + 50 sq. feet = 68 sq. feet
D. 72 sq. feet + 15 sq. feet = 87 sq. feet

4. A school has following space for meditation room. Find the area of the room.

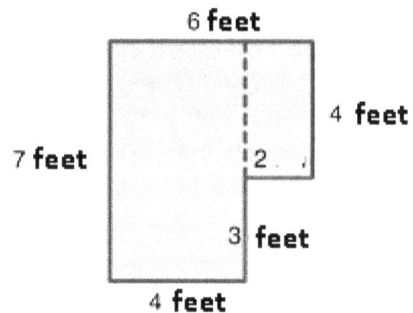

6 feet

4 feet

7 feet

2

3 feet

4 feet

A. 28 sq. feet + 8 sq. feet = 33 sq. feet
B. 72 sq. feet + 50 sq. feet = 122 sq. feet
C. 28 sq. feet + 8 sq. feet = 36 sq. feet
D. 72 sq. feet + 15 sq. feet = 87 sq. feet

5. Find the area of the following shape.

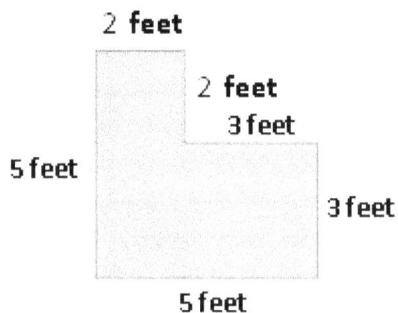

2 feet

2 feet

3 feet

5 feet

3 feet

5 feet

A. 10 sq. feet + 9 sq. feet = 19 sq. feet
B. 72 sq. feet + 50 sq. feet = 122 sq. feet
C. 28 sq. feet + 8 sq. feet = 36 sq. feet
D. 72 sq. feet + 15 sq. feet = 87 sq. feet

PROBLEM SET 62

3.6D decompose composite figures formed by rectangles into non-overlapping rectangles to determine the area of the original figure using the additive property of area.

1. A school has following space for visitors' room. Find the area of the room.

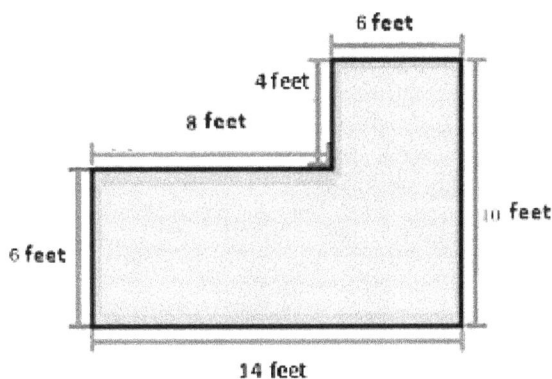

6 **feet**
4 feet
8 feet
10 feet
6 feet
14 feet

A. 50 sq. feet + 209 sq. feet = 70 sq. feet
B. 60 sq. feet + 48 sq. feet = 108 sq. feet
C. 74 sq. feet + 60 sq. feet = 134 sq. feet
D. 48 sq. feet + 140 sq. feet = 188 sq. feet

2. Sam has the following space for his dining and living room. Find the area.

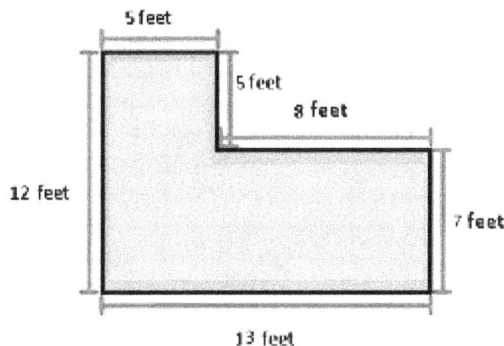

5 feet
5 feet
8 feet
12 feet
7 feet
13 feet

A. 50 sq. feet + 209 sq. feet = 70 sq. feet
B. 60 sq. feet + 40 sq. feet = 100 sq. feet
C. 60 sq. feet + 56 sq. feet = 116 sq. feet
D. 50 sq. feet + 56 sq. feet = 106 sq. feet

3. Peter bought a land for his shop. To buy a carpet he needs to know the area. Find the area.

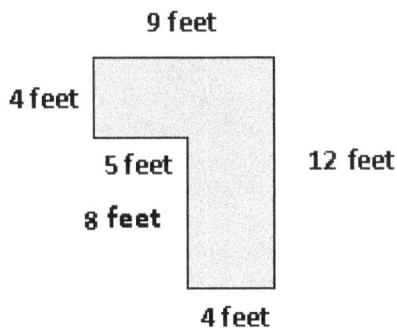

9 feet
4 feet
5 feet
12 feet
8 feet
4 feet

A. 48 sq. feet + 40 sq. feet = 88 sq. feet
B. 36 sq. feet + 32 sq. feet = 68 sq. feet
C. 36 sq. feet + 48 sq. feet = 84 sq. feet
D. 36 sq. feet + 42 sq. feet = 78 sq. feet

4. Harry's has a lawn. He wants to plant some flowers but he needs to know the area. Help him in calculating the area.

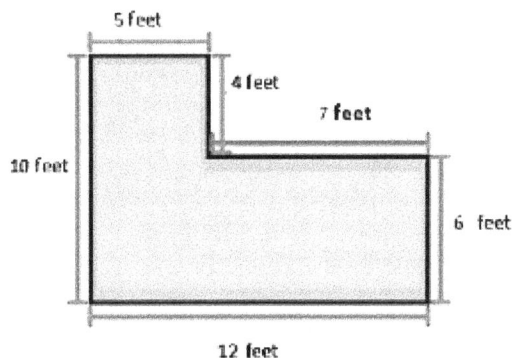

5 feet
4 feet
7 feet
10 feet
6 feet
12 feet

A. 120 sq. feet + 42 sq. feet = 162 sq. feet
B. 50 sq. feet + 35 sq. feet = 85 sq. feet
C. 70 sq. feet + 60 sq. feet = 130 sq. feet
D. 50 sq. feet + 42 sq. feet = 92 sq. feet

5. A dance room has following shape. Tia wants to know the area of the room so that she can buy carpet for the room. Help Tia to calculate the area.

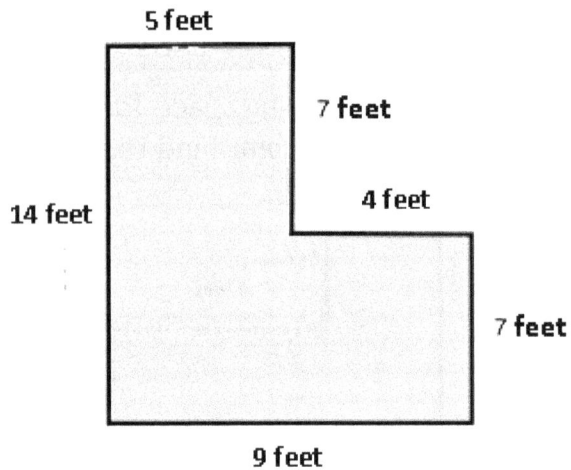

5 feet

7 feet

4 feet

14 feet

7 feet

9 feet

A. 70 sq. feet + 28 sq. feet = 98 sq. feet
B. 14 sq. feet + 35 sq. feet = 49 sq. feet
C. 70 sq. feet + 63 sq. feet = 133 sq. feet
D. $14 \times 5 \times 7 = 490$ sq. feet

PROBLEM SET 63

3.6E *decompose two congruent two-dimensional figures into parts with equal areas and express the area of each part as a unit fraction of the whole and recognize that equal shares of identical wholes need not have the same shape.*

1. Which fraction shows the fraction?

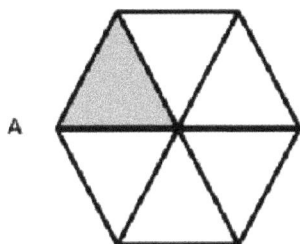

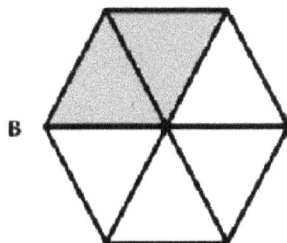

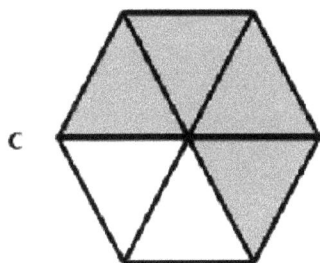

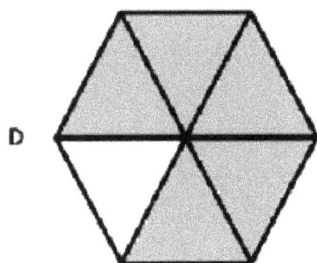

A

B

C

D

2. What fraction of the shape is pink?

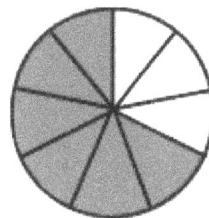

A. $\frac{1}{6}$

B. $\frac{6}{7}$

C. $\frac{6}{9}$

D. $\frac{6}{8}$

3. What fraction of the shape is green?

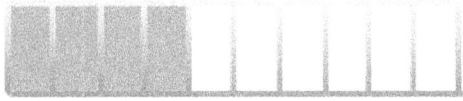

A. $\dfrac{4}{10}$

B. $\dfrac{6}{9}$

C. $\dfrac{8}{10}$

D. $\dfrac{6}{10}$

4. Which fraction shows the fraction ?

A

B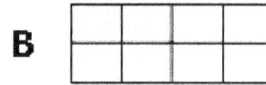

C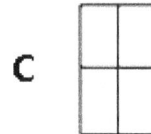

D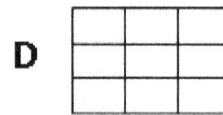

5. Which fraction shows the fraction ?

A

B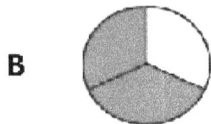

C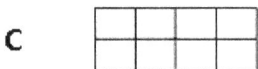

D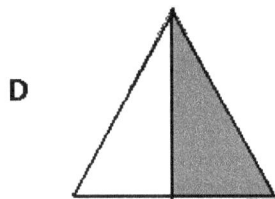

3.6E *decompose two congruent two-dimensional figures into parts with equal areas and express the area of each part as a unit fraction of the whole and recognize that equal shares of identical wholes need not have the same shape.*

1. What fraction of the shape is yellow?

A. $\dfrac{4}{5}$

B. $\dfrac{1}{4}$

C. $\dfrac{2}{4}$

D. $\dfrac{3}{4}$

2. Which fraction shows the fraction ?

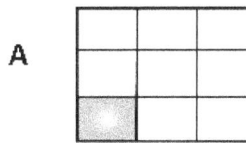

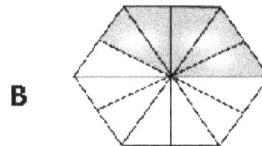

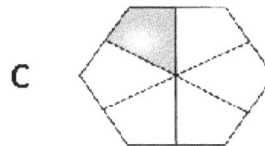

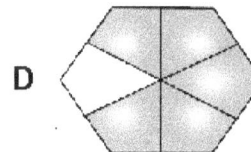

A

B

C

D

3. Which fraction shows the fraction ?

A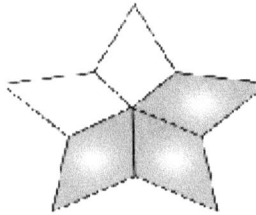

B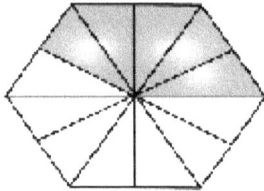

C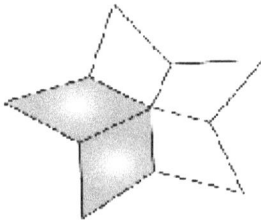

D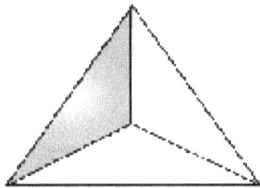

4. Which fraction shows the fraction ?

A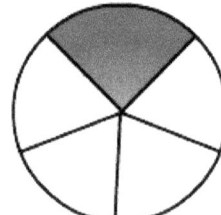

B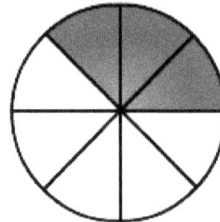

C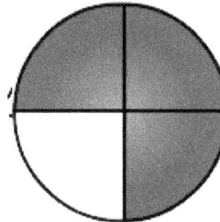

D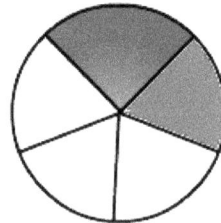

5. What fraction of the shape is yellow?

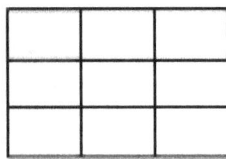

A. $\frac{4}{5}$

B. $\frac{3}{6}$

C. $\frac{3}{9}$

D. $\frac{3}{8}$

PROBLEM SET 65

> **3.7A** *Represent fractions of halves, fourths, and eighths as distances from zero on a number line.*

1. What fraction is represented by A of the following line?

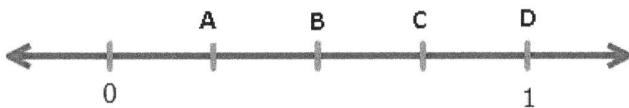

A   B   C   D

0 ———————————————— 1

A. $\frac{1}{2}$

B. $\frac{1}{3}$

C. $\frac{1}{4}$

D. $\frac{2}{4}$

2. What fraction is represented by D of the following line?

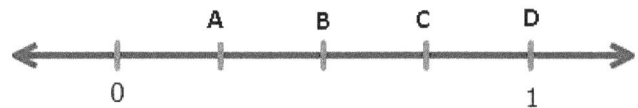

A   B   C   D

0 ———————————————— 1

A. $\frac{1}{2}$

B. $\frac{1}{3}$

C. $\frac{1}{4}$

D. $\frac{4}{4}$

3. What fraction is represented by B of the following line?

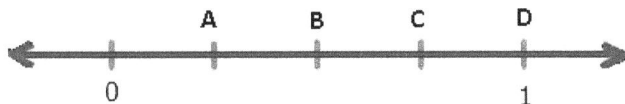

A   B   C   D

0 ———————————————— 1

A. one half
B. One third
C. One fourth
D. Two third

4. What fraction is represented by C of the following line?

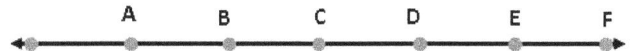

A   B   C   D   E   F

A. $\frac{1}{6}$

B. $\frac{2}{6}$

C. $\frac{3}{6}$

D. $\frac{5}{6}$

5. On which point on the number line the number one-third belongs?

A. On 0
B. On A
C. On B
D. On 1

PROBLEM SET 66

3.7A Represent fractions of halves, fourths, and eighths as distances from zero on a number line.

1. What fraction is represented by C of the following line?

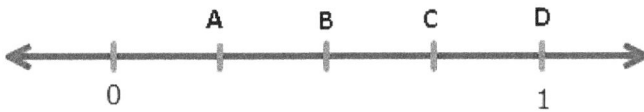

A. $\frac{1}{2}$

B. $\frac{1}{3}$

C. $\frac{1}{4}$

D. $\frac{3}{4}$

2. What fraction is represented by B of the following line?

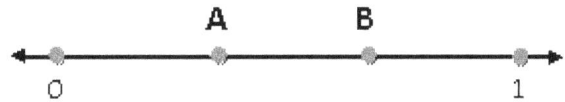

A. Haves
B. One third
C. One fourth
D. Two third

3. What fraction is represented by E of the following line?

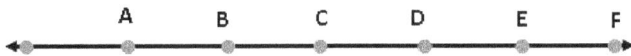

A. $\frac{1}{6}$

B. $\frac{2}{6}$

C. $\frac{3}{6}$

D. $\frac{5}{6}$

4. Which of the following number lines is divided into quarters only?

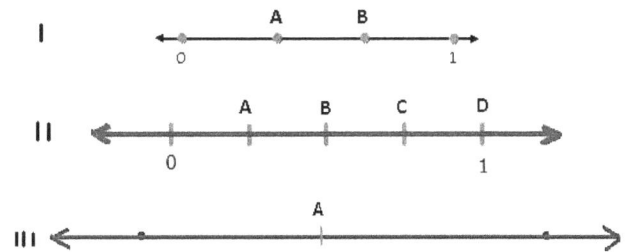

A. I
B. II
C. III
D. None of these

5. Which of the following number lines is divided into fourths only?

I
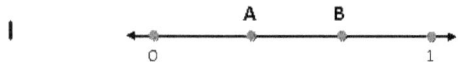

II
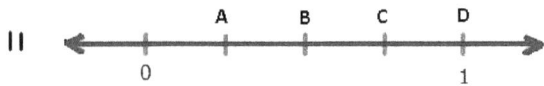

III
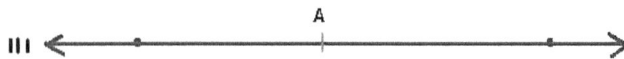

A. I
B. II
C. III
D. None of these

PROBLEM SET 67

3.7B determine the perimeter of a polygon or a missing length when given perimeter and remaining side lengths in problems.

1. Think of a baby doll starting from one corner of a small box, and walking all the way round the edge - what distance will it have walked?

Start

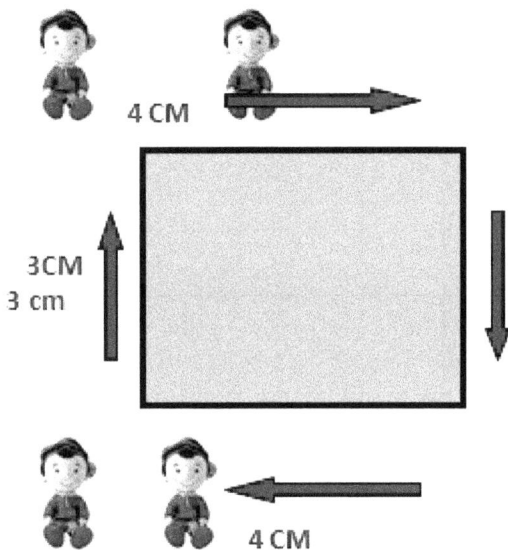

4 CM

3CM
3 cm

4 CM

| First Side – 4CM |
| Second Side – 3CM |
| Third Side – 4CM |
| Fourth Side – 3CM |
| Total |
| =4+3+4+3=14CM |

A. 7 cm
B. 10 cm
C. 14 cm
D. 8 cm

2. Anna has a garden in the following shape. Find the perimeter of the garden.

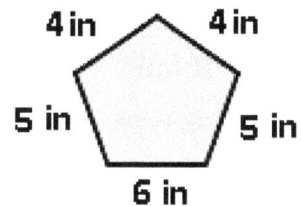

4 in   4 in
5 in   5 in
6 in

A. 16 in
B. 15 in
C. 14 in
D. 24 in

3. Paula has a dancing floor in the shape given below. She is weak in calculation. If the perimeter is 34 km, find the value of k.

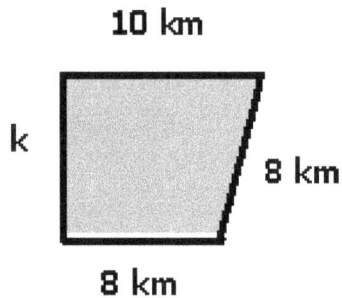

10 km

k

8 km

8 km

A. 8 km
B. 18 km
C. 14 km
D. 26 km

4. Saila has a piece of wood in the shape given below. She needs to know the value of a. Find the value of a if the perimeter is 26 in.

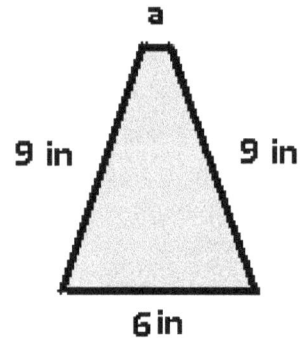

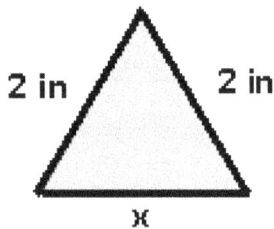

a

9 in   9 in

6 in

A. 4 in
B. 2 in
C. 12 in
D. 6 in

5. Saila has a piece of paper to decorate the party. She wanted to put some pearls on the side of the paper. To do this she needs to know the value of a. Find the value of a if the perimeter is 6 in.

2 in   2 in

x

A. 2 in
B. 6 in
C. 8 in
D. 4 in

PROBLEM SET 68

> 3.7B determine the perimeter of a polygon or a missing length when given perimeter and remaining side lengths in problems.

1. Iliana has a piece of land in which she is planning to plant some trees. She wanted to calculate the perimeter so that she can have an idea about it. To do this she needs to know the value of b. Find the value of b if the perimeter is 30 km.

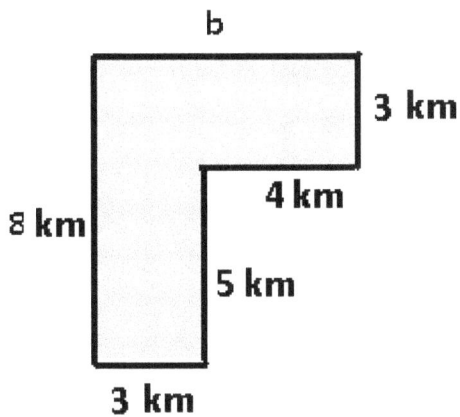

b

3 km

4 km

8 km

5 km

3 km

A. 3 km
B. 4 km
C. 6 km
D. 7 km

2. Sameera is throwing her birthday party for which she is preparing some cards. She needs to know the value of b to stick some beads. Find the value of b if the perimeter of the paper is 42 cm.

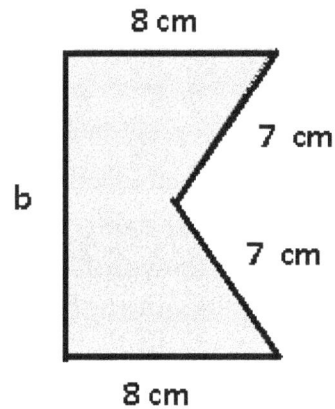

8 cm

7 cm

b

7 cm

8 cm

A. 14 cm
B. 10 cm
C. 12 cm
D. 8 cm

3. Find the value of y if the perimeter of the land is 29 km.

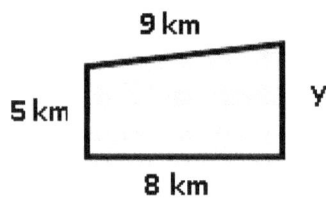

9 km

5 km

y

8 km

A. 6 km
B. 7 km
C. 8 km
D. 9 km

4. Mrs. McArthur needs to purchase some fencing for his land. For that she needs to know the value of x. Find the value of x.

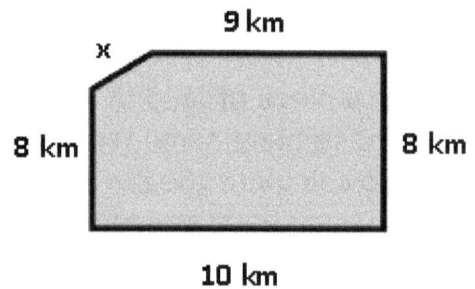

9 km

x

8 km

8 km

10 km

A. 1 km
B. 10 km
C. 8 km
D. 2 km

5. Kaira's rectangular table is 16 centimeters long and 12 centimeters wide. What is its perimeter?

A. 32 cm
B. 44 cm
C. 28 cm
D. 56 cm

PROBLEM SET 69

3.7C determine the solutions to problems involving addition and subtraction of time intervals in minutes using pictorial models or tools such as a 15-minute event plus a 30-minute event equals 45 minutes.

1. Jessica puts cookies in the oven at 6:50 A.M. First she needs to cook for 18 minutes and then 20 minutes more. What time should Jessica take the cookies out of the oven?

A. 6:28 A.M.
B. 7:18 A.M.
C. 7:28 A.M.
D. 7:38 A.M.

2. Riya rents a movie that is 1 hour and 24 minutes long. She starts watching the movie at 3:00 P.M. What time will the movie end?

A. 4:28 P.M.
B. 7:18 P.M.
C. 7:28 P.M.
D. 4:24 P.M.

3. Paul and Nora worked on a project from 5:00 P.M. to 7:13 P.M. How long did they work on the project?

A. One hour and thirteen minutes
B. Three hours and thirteen minutes
C. Two hours and thirteen minutes
D. Two hours and three minutes

4. Cassandra's watch says it is 4:20 P.M. She will go to dinner in 4 hours and 20 minutes. What time will she go to dinner?

A. 8:20 P.M.
B. 8:40 P.M.
C. 7:40 P.M.
D. 8:50 P.M.

5. Andrew walked to school, this morning, at

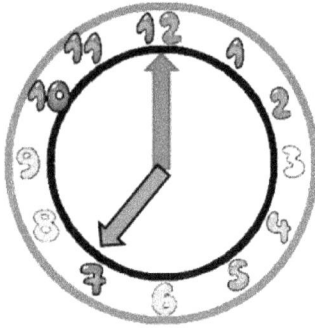

It took Andrew thirty minutes to walk to school gate and ten minutes more to reach his class What time did Andrew arrive at school?

A. 7:40 P.M.
B. 7:20 A.M.
C. 7:30 A.M.
D. 7:40 A.M.

PROBLEM SET 70

3.7C determine the solutions to problems involving addition and subtraction of time intervals in minutes using pictorial models or tools such as a 15-minute event plus a 30-minute event equals 45 minutes.

1. Leon went over to a friend's house to play. She arrived at her friend's house at six o'clock and stayed for one hour and forty minutes. What time was it when Leon went home?

  A. 7:40 P.M.
  B. 7:20 A.M.
  C. 7:30 A.M.
  D. 8:40 P.M.

2. Sam took his car to the shop for an oil change. He dropped the car off at 11:25. Sam came back to pick up her car 2 hours and 40 minutes later. What time was it when he picked up the car?

  A. 1:05 P.M.
  B. 1:20 A.M.
  C. 2:05 A.M.
  D. 2:10 P.M.

3. The TV show Kyle watched ended at

This afternoon, Kyle watched one hour twenty minute TV show. What time did the TV show begin?

A. 6:10 A.M.
B. 5:10 P.M.
C. 6:10 P.M.
D. 6:15 P.M.

4. Rosy started cooking sauce at 12:15 P.M. It must cook for 1 hour and 20 minutes. When will the sauce be ready?

A. 1:25 P.M.
B. 1:35 P.M.
C. 2:35 P.M.
D. 1:45 P.M.

5. Larissa had a terrible cold. She fell asleep at five past nine and slept for a long time. The phone woke her up twenty-one hours and fifty-five minutes later. What time was it when Larissa woke up?

A. Ten to seven
B. Twenty to seven
C. Six o'clock
D. Seven o'clock

> 3.7D determine when it is appropriate to use measurements of liquid volume (capacity) or weight.

1. Which is the better estimate for the volume of a baby food jar?

A. 5 fluid ounces
B. 5 liters
C. 5 gram
D. None of the above

2. Which is the better estimate for the volume of a catch up bottle?

A. 1 milliliters
B. 5 milliliters
C. 500 milliliters
D. None of the above

3. Laura has 2 kiloliter water in the tank. To empty the tank, she took a 500 milliliter bucket and started watering the plants. How many full buckets will it take to remove all the water from the tank?

A. 3
B. 4
C. 5
D. None of the above

4. Which is the better estimate for the volume of a bucket?

A. 4 liters
B. 2 liter
C. 10 kilo gram
D. 10 liter

5. Which is closer to the volume of a vinegar bottle?

A. 5 liters
B. 5 gram
C. 500 milliliters
D. None of the above

PROBLEM SET 72

> 3.7D determine when it is appropriate to use measurements of liquid volume (capacity) or weight.

1. Kaira has 10 liters of ice tea on one hot afternoon. If she sells 7 liters, how many will she have left?

   A. 3 liters
   B. 2 gram
   C. 7 liters
   D. 4 liters

2. The doctor prescribed Laila a 210 ml bottle of medicine with the instructions to take 5 ml twice a day. How long does the medicine last?

   A. One week
   B. Two weeks
   C. Three weeks
   D. Four weeks

3. The capacity of a table spoon is about

   A. 150ml
   B. 15ml
   C. 5ml
   D. 50ml

4. The capacity of a medium sized car's fuel tank is about

   A. 5liters
   B. 5liters l
   C. 50liters
   D. None of the above

5. Which is the better estimate for the volume of a Keith's ink bottle?

   A. 200ml
   B. 50liters
   C. 600ml
   D. 5ml

PROBLEM SET 73

3.7E determine liquid volume (capacity) or weight using appropriate units and tools.

1. Sarah bought some juice containers. She is unable to decide about the volume of juice. Which is a better estimate for the volume of a juice container?

   A. 1 liters
   B. 1 milliliters
   C. 1 gram
   D. None of the above

2. Dora got a bottle of nail polish on her birthday. She wanted to know about its volume. Which is a better estimate for the volume of a bottle of nail polish?

   A. 8 kilogram
   B. 8 liters
   C. 8 milliliters
   D. None of the above

3. Mom is preparing morning tea for everyone. Jack came in the kitchen and eager to know the volume of the tea pot. Which is a better estimate for the volume of a tea pot?

   A. 2 milliliters
   B. 2 liters
   C. 2 gram
   D. None of the above

4. Which is a better estimate for the volume of an ear dropper?

   A. 4 liters
   B. 2 gram
   C. 2 kilo gram
   D. 4 milliliters

5. Which is closer to the volume of a bathtub?

   A. 2 liters
   B. 2 gram
   C. 200 liters
   D. None of the above

3.7E determine liquid volume (capacity) or weight using appropriate units and tools.

1. Dora has 38 liters of soda, and Julie has 44 liters of soda. How many liters of soda do they have in all?

A. 82 liters
B. 82 gram
C. 80 liters
D. 92 liters

2. Paula drinks 475 ml juice from 1 liter container. How much juice is left in the container?

A. 550ml
B. 575ml
C. 525ml
D. 580ml

3. Morgan removed 450ml of water from his fish bowl. If he left 125ml of water in the fish bowl how much water did it have to begin with?

A. 570ml
B. 575ml
C. 475ml
D. 580ml

4. A jug holds 500ml of juice. After I pour a glass there is 425ml of juice left in the jug. How much juice did I pour into my glass?

A. 70ml
B. 50ml
C. 75ml
D. 80ml

5. I bought three cartons of milk. Each carton held 250ml of milk. How much milk did I buy in all?

A. 750ml
B. 500ml
C. 600
D. 900

PROBLEM SET 75

3.4C Determine the value of a collection of coins and bills.

1. Kaif went to the shop with the following coins. How much money is there with Kaif?

   A. 4¢
   B. 5¢
   C. 20¢
   D. 10¢

2. Jessica found some coins in her drawer while cleaning it. How much money is there in the drawer?

   A. 4¢
   B. 5¢
   C. 10¢
   D. 6¢

3. The grandmother gave Kitty some coins as shown below. How much money is there?

   A. 14¢
   B. 16¢
   C. 10¢
   D. 6¢

4. Saira got some coins from her mom for buying some chocolates. How much money is there?

   A. $0.75
   B. $1.75
   C. $0.50
   D. $0.60

5. A painter went to the store to get supplies. She spent $55 on paint and $85 on brushes. How much did she spend in all?

   A. $130
   B. $140
   C. $150
   D. $160

REPORTING CATEGORY 4 *(SUPPORTING)*
DATA ANALYSIS &
PERSONAL FINANCIAL LITERACY

PROBLEM SET 76

3.4C Determine the value of a collection of coins and bills.

1. Sam and Ali went to an ice cream shop together. Sam's waffle cone cost $3.25, and Ali's hot fudge sundae cost $4.75. How much was their bill?

A. $8.00
B. $7.50
C. $7.25
D. $8.50

2. Pooh wants to eat ice cream. How many quarters does she need to buy an ice cream?

$1.75

A. 5
B. 6
C. 7
D. 8

3. Sonia buys a pair of green shoes and a red wallet. The cost of green shoes is $10.50 and the cost of red wallet is $3.75. She has a coupon worth $12.75. How much money does she need to pay?

A. $0.75
B. $0.50
C. $1.25
D. $1.50

4. Alefiya had $20. She bought a green handbag. The price of green bag is $8.25. How much money does she have left?

A. $11.75
B. $10.50
C. $11.25
D. $12.50

5. Grandfather gave some money to Jack to buy some items. Jack bought 1 box of cookies, 1 bottle jam and 1 bottle juice. How much did Jack pay to the shopkeeper?

Milk $ 9.40   Jam $ 4.50   Juice $2.25   Cookies $3.75   Honey $ 5.60

A. $11.75
B. $10.50
C. $11.25
D. $12.50

> *3.8A summarize a data set with multiple categories using a frequency table, dot plot, pictograph, or bar graph with scaled intervals.*

1. Look at the following table:

Donations		
Person	Clea Water	Orphan education
Sonia	$87	$56
Anne	$105	$67
Katrina	$117	$89

How much more did Katrina donate to clean water than to Orphan education?

A. 18   **B.** 22

C. 28   **D.** 38

2. Look at the following table:

Movie ticket prices		
Movie	Child	Senior
Michigan	$6	$7
Oakland	$7	$9
California	$9	$12
Central Park	$4	$6
Seattle	$6	$7

How much more does a senior ticket cost at the California movie than at the Seattle movie?

A. $7   **B.** $6

C. $4   **D.** $5

3. Look at the following bar graph.

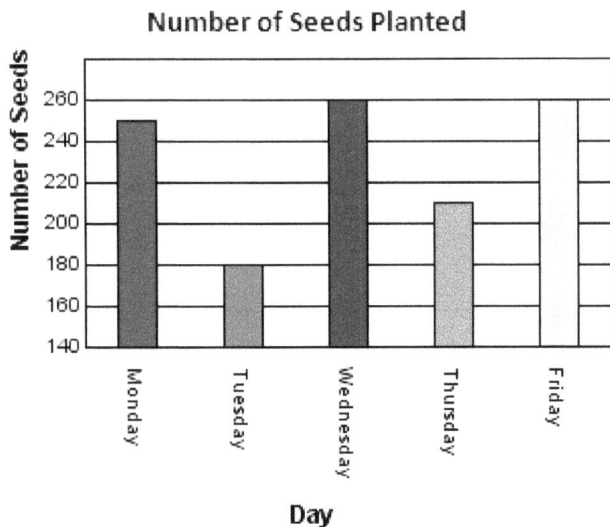

Number of Seeds Planted

How many more seeds were planted on Friday than on Tuesday?

A. 70   **B.** 80

C. 60   **D.** 40

4. Look at the following bar graph.

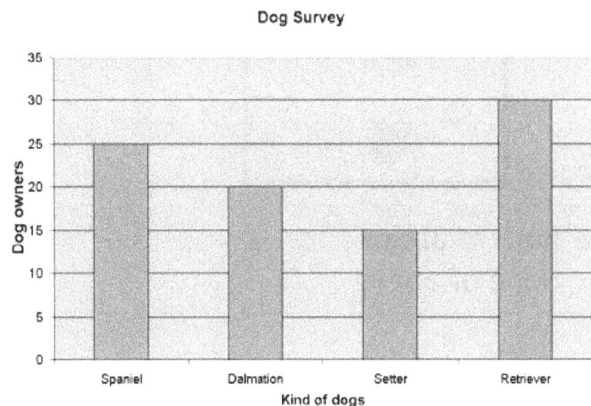

Dog Survey

Which breed of dog owner is most?

A. Spaniel   **B.** Dalmatian

C. Setter   **D.** Retriever

5. Look at the picture:

Which table shows the number of cakes, cupcakes and apples correctly?

A

B

C. Both of above

D. None of above

PROBLEM SET 78

3.8A summarize a data set with multiple categories using a frequency table, dot plot, pictograph, or bar graph with scaled intervals.

1. Kaira asked people how many letters they wrote last year.

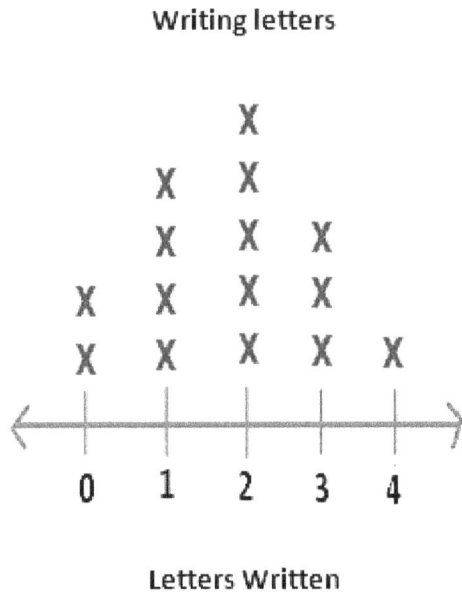

Writing letters

```
              X
        X     X
        X     X     X
  X     X     X     X
  X     X     X     X     X
<─┼─────┼─────┼─────┼─────┼─>
  0     1     2     3     4
```

Letters Written

How many people wrote exactly 3 letters?

A. 3
B. 4
C. 5
D. 6

2. John and his friends were comparing the amount of pieces cakes they received on Christmas. They recorded their information in the pictograph below.

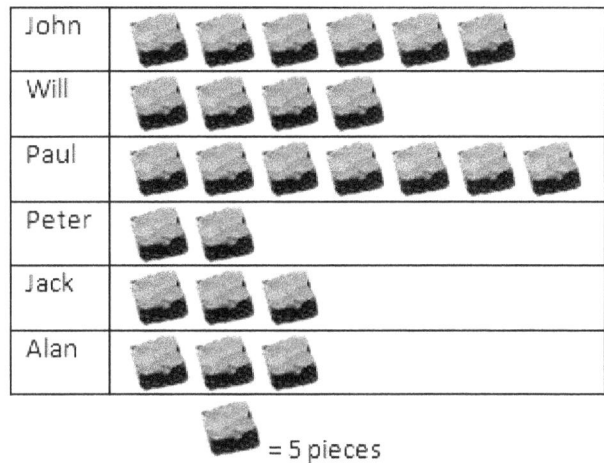

John	🍰🍰🍰🍰🍰🍰
Will	🍰🍰🍰🍰
Paul	🍰🍰🍰🍰🍰🍰🍰
Peter	🍰🍰
Jack	🍰🍰🍰
Alan	🍰🍰🍰

🍰 = 5 pieces

How many pieces of cakes did Paul get?

A. 30
B. 45
C. 40
D. 35

3. At a fundraiser students from Mrs. Julia's class were selling popsicles. Mrs. Julia recorded their information in the pictograph below.

Popsicles Sale Results

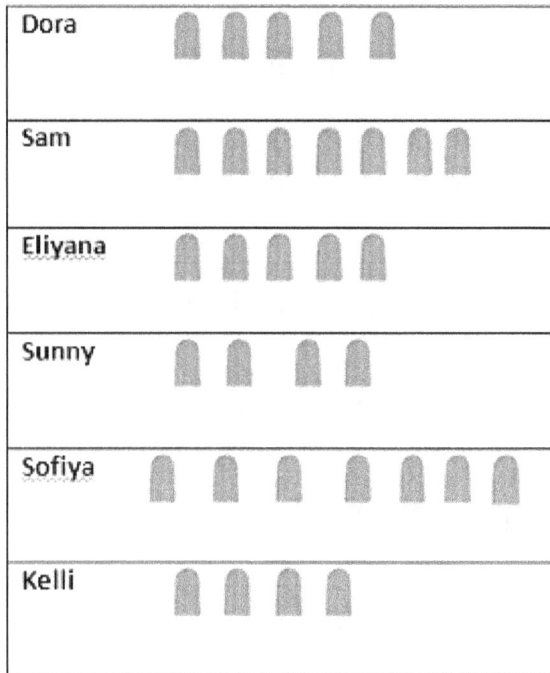

Dora	🍦🍦🍦🍦 🍦
Sam	🍦🍦🍦🍦🍦🍦🍦🍦
Eliyana	🍦🍦🍦🍦
Sunny	🍦🍦 🍦🍦
Sofiya	🍦🍦🍦🍦🍦🍦🍦
Kelli	🍦🍦🍦🍦

🍦 = 2 popsicles sold

How many popsicles did Sofiya sell than Kelli?

A. 14
B. 6
C. 8
D. 4

4. Look at the dot graph below.

Family Size

Number of Children in Family

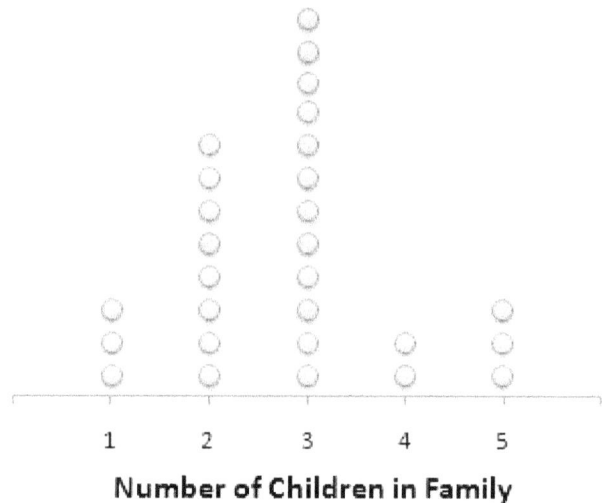

How many families have exactly 2 children?

A. 3
B. 2
C. 8
D. 12

5. The basketball coach looked up how many goals his team members scored last season.

Basketball goals last season

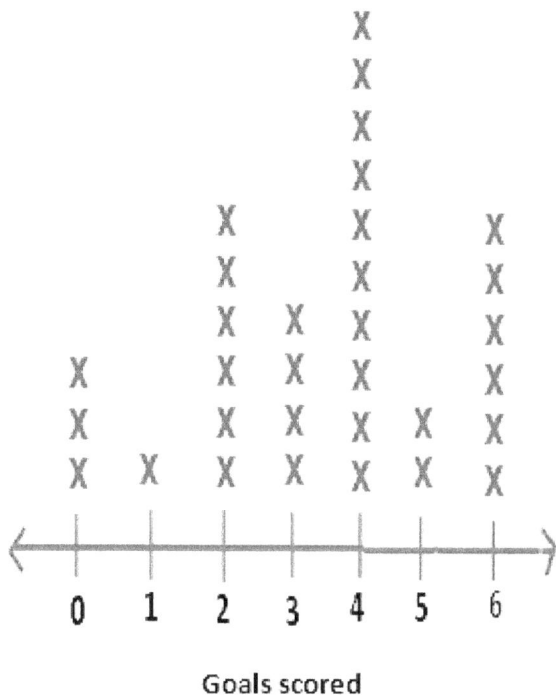

Goals scored

How many team members scored at least 4 goals last season?

A. 14
B. 16
C. 12
D. 18

3.8B solve one- and two-step problems using categorical data represented with a frequency table, dot plot, pictograph, or bar graph with scaled intervals.

1. Karin and her friends recorded their scores while playing a board game.

Scores on a board game	
Score	Frequency
6	18
7	2
8	16
9	7
10	3

How many people scored at least 8?

A. 10
B. 26
C. 24
D. 23

2. The art teacher, Ms. Julie, wrote down how many picture frames the students made last week.

Making picture frames	
Picture frames made	Frequency
0	17
1	15
2	16
3	14
4	20

How many students made more than 2 picture frames?

A. 16
B. 14
C. 34
D. 20

3. The dietician conducted a survey about the favorite juice of a student. She represented the data in bar graph.

Students' Favorite Juices

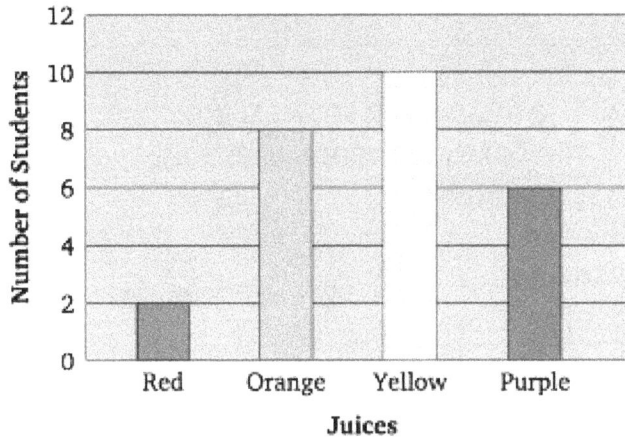

How many more students like yellow juice than red juice?

A. 6
B. 7
C. 8
D. 10

4. The sports teacher recorded the favorite sports of the students and represented by the bar graph below.

Our Favorite Sports

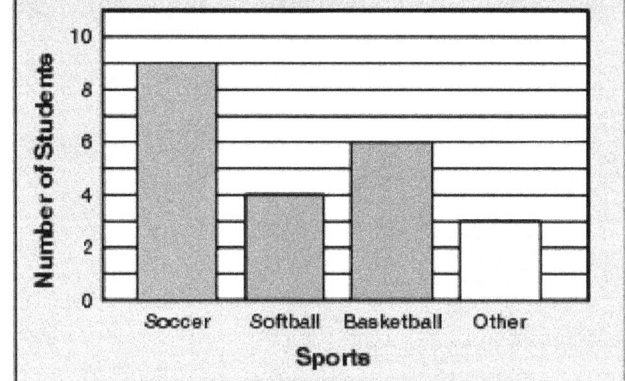

How many more students like soccer than softball?

A. 6
B. 5
C. 4
D. 3

5. Ronita went in a zoo and jotted down the number of animals she saw.

Animals

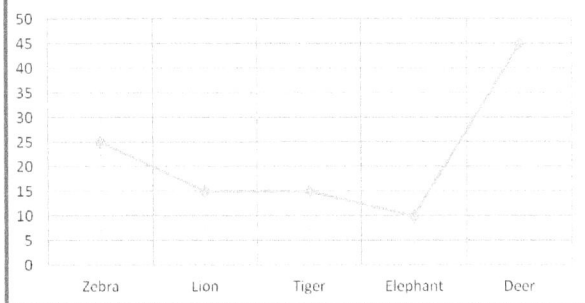

How many more deers than elephants did Ronita see?

A. 15
B. 10
C. 5
D. 35

3.8B solve one- and two-step problems using categorical data represented with a frequency table, dot plot, pictograph, or bar graph with scaled intervals.

1. A grocery store tracked how many mangoes it sold each day.

Mango Sold

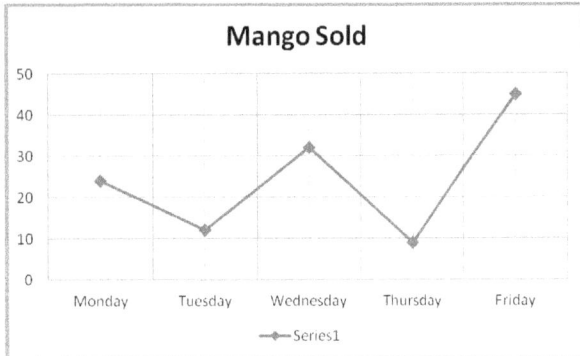

What is the difference of mangoes sale between Tuesday and Wednesday?

A. 30
B. 10
C. 20
D. 1

2. The pictograph shows the number of the boxes of French fries sold by a restaurant:

Monday	
Tuesday	
Wednesday	
Thursday	
Friday	
Saturday	

1 🍟 = 10 boxes

How many more boxes sold on Thursday than Monday?

A. 60
B. 2
C. 10
D. 20

3. Look at this pictograph:

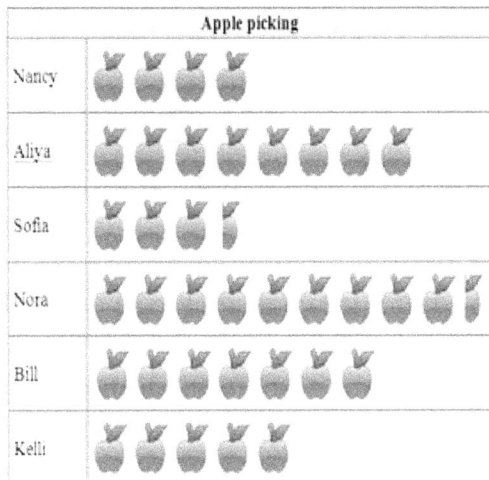

Apple picking

Nancy	🍎🍎🍎
Aliya	🍎🍎🍎🍎🍎🍎
Sofia	🍎🍎🍎🍎
Nora	🍎🍎🍎🍎🍎🍎🍎🍎🍎
Bill	🍎🍎🍎🍎🍎🍎
Kelli	🍎🍎🍎🍎🍎

Each 🍎 = 10 apples

Each 🍎 = 5 apples

How many more apples did Nora pick than Aliya?

A. 15   B. 95
C. 25   D. 10

4. Some students were surveyed about how many pairs of shocks they own.

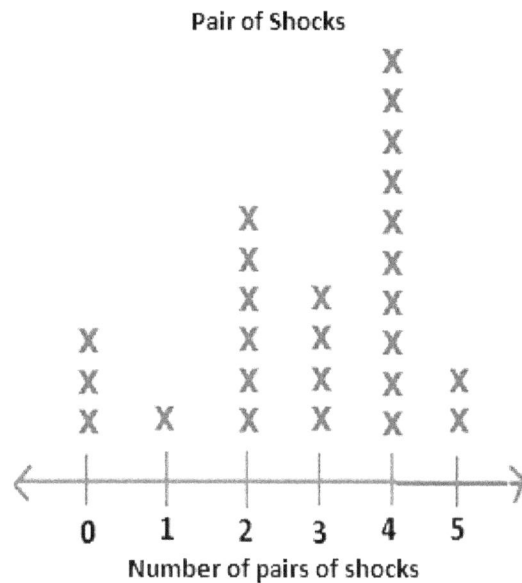

Pair of Shocks

Number of pairs of shocks

How many students own more than 2 pairs of shocks?

A. 15   B. 16
C. 14   D. 12

5. Some friends compared how many times they visited movie theatre last year.

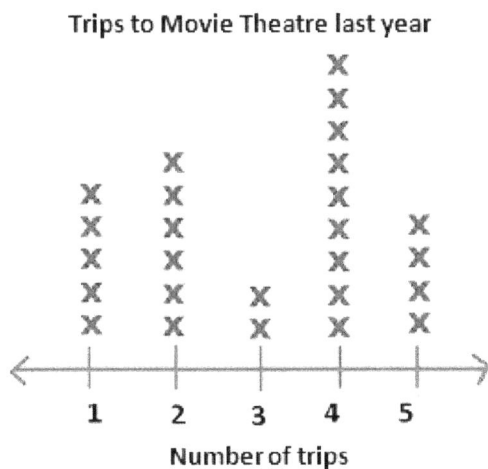

Trips to Movie Theatre last year

Number of trips

How many more people visited 4 times than 3 times?

A. 9   B. 2
C. 7   D. 11

3.9A explain the connection between human capital/labor and income.

---

1. Jessica's mom wanted to teach Jessica the value of money. She told Jessica if she helps her mom in the kitchen everyday for one hour, she will get $10 per hour as hourly wages. Jessica helped her mom every day except Sunday. How much Jessica will get as her wages in one week?

   A. $10
   B. $50
   C. $60
   D. $40

2. You and a friend decide to go into business. You decide to sell lemonade. The frozen lemonade costs $1.50 a can, and 1 can will make 10 cups of lemonade. You and your friend buy and prepare 2 cans of frozen lemonade, and you decide to sell the lemonade for $0.50 a cup. How many cups of lemonade do you and your friend need to sell to cover the cost of the 2 cans of frozen lemonade?

   A. 9
   B. 8
   C. 7
   D. 6

3. You and a friend decide to go into business. You decide to sell lemonade. The frozen lemonade costs $1.50 a can, and 1 can will make 10 cups of lemonade. You and your friend buy and prepare 2 cans of frozen lemonade, and you decide to sell the lemonade for $.50 a cup. How much money is the most you can make together if you sell all of the lemonade?

   A. $10
   B. $9
   C. $8
   D. $7

4. Julia's mom is expert in baking. She makes cake for parties. She decides to make money by selling cake. The ingredients of cake cost $6 for preparing one cake. If she cuts the cake into 10 pieces and sells each piece for $1.50, how much money she will earn by selling one cake after paying for ingredients?

   A. $15
   B. $9
   C. $12
   D. $21

5. Julia's mom is expert in baking. She makes cake for parties. She decides to make money by selling cake. The ingredients of cake cost $6 for preparing one cake. If she cuts the cake into 10 pieces and sells each piece for $1.50, how much money she will earn by selling one cake after paying for ingredients?

A. $15
B. $9
C. $12
D. $21

PROBLEM SET 82

> 9A explain the connection between human capital/labor and income.

1. If Lara finds a $6.50 bill, and she washes a car and waters the plants 2 times, how much money will Lara now have?

A. $10
B. $15
C. $12
D. $16

2. Laila has earned $21.50 and walks the dogs 2 more times. How much will Laila have earned now?

A. $30.50
B. $2.50
C. $29.50
D. $30

3. Sarah is good in baking. She makes cookies for parties. She decided to make money by selling cookies. The ingredients of cookies cost $4 for preparing 20 cookies. If she makes 100 cookies and sells each piece for $0.50, how much money she will earn by selling cookies?

A. $20
B. $30
C. $40
D. $25

4. If Zara waters the plant($4.00) and washes 2 cars ($11), how many times she must wash the clothes to earn $24?

A. 4
B. 5
C. 3
D. 6

5. Shailly mom runs a beauty parlor. She charges $12 for hair cutting. How many times she must cut the hair to earn $84?

A. 8
B. 5
C. 6
D. 7

> *3.9B describe the relationship between the availability or scarcity of resources and how that impacts cost.*

1. In 2014, in Rana's farm, there were 250 kg of apples grown. At that time the average cost of 1 kg was $9 per kg. When went to sell his apples in the market he came to know that the consumption of apples are only 200 kg. Select suitable option from the list below:

A. Rana will sell his apples in lower price.
B. Rana will sell his apples in higher price.
C. Rana will not sell his apples.
D. None of the above.

2. In 2015, in Rana's farm, there were 150 kg of apples grown. At that time the average cost of 1 kg was $9 per kg. When went to sell his apples in the market he came to know that the consumption of apples are only 200 kg. Select suitable option from the list below:

A. Rana will sell his apples in lower price.
B. Rana will sell his apples in higher price.
C. Rana will not sell his apples.
D. None of the above.

3. Jenny's mom works in a vegetable farm. In that farm, last year 500 kg more potatoes were grown. Now the supply of the potatoes are more than the demand. Select suitable option from the list below:

A. The price of the potatoes will be lower.
B. The price of the potatoes will be higher.
C. The price will remain same.
D. None of the above.

4. In 2012, avian flu wiped out millions of chickens in Mexico creating a scarcity of eggs. In this situation the price of the eggs will be _____

A. lower
B. higher
C. stable
D. None of the above

5. Each year a limited amount of the flu vaccine is available to the population, meaning there is not enough for each individual to be vaccinated. This is _____

A. availability
B. market
C. scarcity
D. None of the above

3.9B describe the relationship between the availability or scarcity of resources and how that impacts cost.

1. In 2015, cherries are produce in huge quantity in Harry's farm. What do you think the cost of the cherries will be _____

A. lower
B. higher
C. can't be predicted
D. None of the above

2. An educated population in a country that needs high level skilled workers can result in a _____

A. scarcity of labor
B. demand of labor
C. availability of educated labor
D. None of the above

3. The consumption of potatoes is 1000 tons in the market at the rate of $4 per kg. The farmers grown 2000 tons potatoes this season. What do you think the price of potatoes should be _____

A. $8 per kg
B. $6 per kg
C. $4 per kg
D. $2 per kg

4. In 2015, mangoes are produce in huge quantity in Harry's farm. What do you think the cost of the mango will be _____

A. lower
B. higher
C. can't be predicted
D. None of the above

5. In 2015, mangoes are produce in huge quantity in Harry's farm. What do you think the cost of the mango will be _____

A. lower
B. higher
C. can't be predicted
D. None of the above

PROBLEM SET 85

3.9D explain that credit is used when wants or needs exceed the ability to pay and that it is the borrower's responsibility to pay it back to the lender, usually with interest.

---

1. _____ is money which is added on to the borrowed amount.

A. loan
B. Interest
C. Credit
D. Deposit

2. Laila spent $120 at a music store and paid with a credit card. The credit card company charged $18 in interest on the purchase. What was the total amount Laila paid the credit card company for the purchase?

A. 128
B. 118
C. 138
D. 228

---

3. Warren has $20 to spend. Which of the following can he afford?

A. A dinner out that costs $14
B. A trip to the amusement park that costs $30
C. A $21 donation to a charity
D. A shirt that costs $25

4. Last week, Corony got a check from her grandmother for his birthday and earned a weekly allowance. He spent some of his birthday money on a new skirt, and she bought snacks in the school cafeteria twice with her own money. Identify the correct option about her birthday check.

A. Money increased
B. Money decreased
C. No changes in her money
D. None of the above

---

5. Last week, Corony got a check from her grandmother for his birthday and earned a weekly allowance. He spent some of his birthday money on a new skirt, and she bought snacks in the school cafeteria twice with her own money. Identify the correct option about her birthday check.

A. Money increased
B. Money decreased
C. No changes in her money
D. None of the above

> *3.9D explain that credit is used when wants or needs exceed the ability to pay and that it is the borrower's responsibility to pay it back to the lender, usually with interest.*

1. Which word best describes the money a credit card company charges the cardholder when the amount owed is not paid back immediately?

   A. Deposit
   B. Withdrawal
   C. Loan
   D. Interest

2. Which word best describes the money a credit card company charges the cardholder when the amount owed is not paid back immediately?

   A. Deposit
   B. Withdrawal
   C. Loan
   D. Interest

3. Sarah invested $2000 in her bank account. After one year the amount increased to $2200. How much account she will receive at the end of five years?

   A. $3000
   B. $300
   C. $3200
   D. $3000

4. Saila spent $150 at a grocery store and paid with a credit card. The credit card company charged $25 in interest on the purchase. What was the total amount Saila paid the credit card company for the purchase?

   A. 155
   B. 115
   C. 175
   D. 275

5. Alefiya makes clothing for a store. Recently she made some dresses. The fabric cost $240. The pattern, zipper, buttons, and thread cost $120. She charges $10 as interest on total amount. How much did it cost Alefiya to make the dresses?

   A. $360
   B. $370
   C. $270
   D. $260

> 3.9E list reasons to save and explain the benefit of a savings plan, including for college.

1. You have $136.50 in your savings account. If you withdraw $40, how much will you have left in your savings account?

   A. $166.50
   B. $195.50
   C. $186.50
   D. $196.50

2. Every month, the bank pays you for keeping money in your savings account. What is this?

   A. Saving
   B. Interest
   C. Profit
   D. None of the above

3. You have $341.50 in your savings account. You want to buy a shoe for you. The cost of the shoe is $17. If you withdraw $17, how much will you have left in your savings account?

   A. $324.50
   B. $325.50
   C. $234.50
   D. $236.50

4. What is money?

   A. A paper
   B. Paper to buy things
   C. A currency
   D. None of the above

5. How will you earn extra money to save for future?

   A. Mowing lawns
   B. Cleaning yards
   C. Shoveling snow
   D. All of the above

PROBLEM SET 88

3.9E list reasons to save and explain the benefit of a savings plan, including for college.

1. Laura did a bake sale in her school. She baked cupcakes which costs $2. If she sold 46 cupcakes, how much money did she earn?

   A. $82.00
   B. $94.00
   C. $92.00
   D. $72.00

2. You have $154 in your account. Next week you'll deposit a check for $34.62. How much will you have in your savings account then?

   A. $188.62
   B. $184.62
   C. $186.62
   D. $198.62

3. Aliya wants to buy a doll house which costs $49. If he earns $7 per day by washing the utensils, in how many days will she earn $49?

   A. 9
   B. 6
   C. 7
   D. 8

4. If Harry wants to wash cars to earn gas money, how many cars must he wash to make at least $75($3 for one car wash)?

   A. 22
   B. 23
   C. 25
   D. 33

5. Alex wants to buy a video game which costs $46. If he earns $2 per day by walking a dog, in how many days will he earn $46?

   A. 21
   B. 23
   C. 25
   D. 33

ANSWER KEY TO ALL PROBLEMS

3.2A Problem Set 1
1. D
2. A
3. A
4. A
5. D

3.2A Problem Set 2
1. C
2. C
3. D
4. C
5. D

3.2B Problem Set 3
1. C
2. 9
3. C
4. B
5. A

3.2B Problem Set 4
1. C
2. D
3. 2,906
4. D
5. A

3.2C Problem Set 5
1. D
2. C
3. C
4. C
5. A

3.2C Problem Set 6
1. D
2. C
3. A
4. D
5. C

3.2D Problem Set 7
1. D
2. B
3. A
4. D
5. B

3.2D Problem Set 8
1. C
2. D
3. B
4. D
5. A

3.3A Problem Set 9
1. C
2. A
3. B
4. C
5. D

3.3A Problem Set 10
1. D
2. B
3. B
4. B
5. A

3.3B Problem Set 11
1. C
2. A
3. D
4. B
5. B

3.3B Problem Set 12
1. C
2. B
3. B
4. D
5. A

3.3C Problem Set 13
1. A
2. A
3. A
4. A
5. C

3.3C Problem Set 14
1. C
2. B
3. C
4. B
5. C

3.3D Problem Set 15
1. B
2. D
3. D
4. A
5. C

3.3D Problem Set 16
1. A
2. C
3. D
4. D
5. B

3.3E Problem Set 17
1. B
2. D
3. C
4. A
5. B

3.3E Problem Set 18
1. A
2. A
3. C
4. A
5. D

3.3F Problem Set 19
1. A
2. C
3. B
4. A
5. D

3.3F Problem Set 20
1. $=$
2. $\neq$
3. B
4. B
5. C

3.3G Problem Set 21
1. C
2. A
3. C
4. A
5. A

3.3G Problem Set 22
1. C
2. C
3. C
4. A
5. D

3.3H Problem Set 23
1. C
2. A
3. D
4. D
5. B

3.3H Problem Set 24
1. C
2. C
3. C
4. B
5. A

3.4I Problem Set 25
1. C
2. B
3. C
4. B
5. B

3.4I Problem Set 26
1. C
2. B
3. B
4. A
5. A

3.4A Problem Set 27
1. C
2. B
3. C
4. B
5. D

3.4A Problem Set 28
1. A
2. D
3. B
4. A
5. D

3.4B Problem Set 29
1. B
2. A
3. B
4. A
5. D

3.4B Problem Set 30
1. C
2. A
3. B
4. A
5. B

3.4D Problem Set31
1. C
2. C
3. C
4. D
5. A

3.4D Problem Set 32
1. B
2. D
3. D
4. C
5. B

3.4E Problem Set 33
1. C
2. B
3. D
4. B
5. C

3.4E Problem Set 34
1. D
2. B
3. A
4. B
5. D

3.4F Problem Set 35
1. D
2. A
3. A
4. C
5. C

3.4F Problem Set 36
1. B
2. A
3. D
4. B
5. C

3.4G Problem Set 37
1. B
2. A
3. D
4. C
5. C

3.4G Problem Set 38
1. B
2. B
3. B
4. A
5. C

3.4H Problem Set 39
1. C
2. D
3. A
4. B
5. C

3.4H Problem Set 40
1. B
2. D
3. A
4. D
5. C

3.4J Problem Set 41
1. C
2. B
3. C
4. C
5. A

3.4J Problem Set 42
1. D
2. D
3. B
4. A
5. A

3.4K Problem Set 43
1. B
2. C
3. C
4. D
5. C

3.4K Problem Set 44
1. A
2. C
3. A
4. C
5. D

3.5A Problem Set 45
1. C
2. B
3. C
4. C
5. B

3.5A Problem Set 46
1. D
2. D
3. A
4. C
5. D

3.5B Problem Set 47
1. C
2. B
3. A
4. B
5. A

3.5B Problem Set 48
1. B
2. C
3. A
4. D
5. B

3.5C Problem Set 49
1. C
2. A
3. D
4. A
5. D

3.5C Problem Set 50
1. C
2. B
3. D
4. B
5. A

3.5D Problem Set 51
1. C
2. B
3. A
4. B
5. A

3.5D Problem Set 52
1. C
2. C
3. B
4. B
5. D

3.5E Problem Set 53
1. B
2. B
3. B
4. D
5. B

3.5E Problem Set 54
1. C
2. A
3. C
4. A
5. C

3.6A Problem Set 55
1. D
2. B
3. C
4. A
5. C

3.6A Problem Set 56
1. D
2. B
3. A
4. D
5. B

3.6B Problem Set 57
1. D
2. C
3. B
4. B
5. B

3.6B Problem Set 58
1. A
2. C
3. D
4. C
5. C

3.6C Problem Set 59

1. C
2. B
3. A
4. A
5. C

3.6C Problem Set 60

1. B
2. B
3. D
4. C
5. C

3.6D Problem Set 61

1. A
2. D
3. B
4. C
5. A

3.6D Problem Set 62

1. B
2. C
3. B
4. D
5. A

3.6E Problem Set 63

1. D
2. C
3. A
4. D
5. B

3.6E Problem Set 64

1. D
2. B
3. C
4. B
5. C

3.7A Problem Set 65

1. C
2. D
3. A
4. C
5. B

3.7A Problem Set 66

1. D
2. D
3. D
4. A
5. B

3.7B Problem Set 67

1. C
2. D
3. A
4. B
5. A

3.7B Problem Set 68

1. D
2. C
3. B
4. A
5. D

3.7C Problem Set 69

1. C
2. D
3. C
4. B
5. D

3.7C Problem Set 70

1. A
2. C
3. C
4. B
5. D

3.7D Problem Set 71

1. A
2. C
3. B
4. D
5. C

3.7D Problem Set 72

1. A
2. C
3. B
4. C
5. A

3.7E Problem Set 73

1. A
2. C
3. B
4. D
5. C

3.7E Problem Set 74

1. A
2. C
3. B
4. C
5. A

3.4C Problem Set 75

1. C
2. D
3. B
4. A
5. B

3.4C Problem Set 76

1. A
2. C
3. D
4. A
5. B

3.8A Problem Set 77

1. C
2. D
3. B
4. D
5. A

3.8A Problem Set 78

1. A
2. D
3. B
4. C
5. D

3.8B Problem Set 79

1. B
2. C
3. C
4. B
5. D

3.8B Problem Set 80

1. C
2. D
3. A
4. B
5. C

3.9A Problem Set 81

1. C
2. D
3. A
4. B
5. D

3.9A Problem Set 82

1. C
2. A
3. B
4. C
5. D

3.9B Problem Set 83
1. A
2. B
3. A
4. B
5. C

3.9B Problem Set 84
1. A
2. C
3. D
4. A
5. B

3.9D Problem Set 85
1. B
2. C
3. A
4. A
5. B

3.9D Problem Set 86
1. D
2. C
3. A
4. C
5. B

3.9E Problem Set 87
1. D
2. B
3. A
4. C
5. D

3.9E Problem Set 88
1. C
2. A
3. C
4. C
5. B

www.ingramcontent.com/pod-product-compliance
Lightning Source LLC
Chambersburg PA
CBHW081513040426
42447CB00013B/3209